CRUSADE IN SPAIN

Eoin O'DUFFY

CRUSADE IN SPAIN

Foreword by
Michael MCCORMACK

Reconquista Press

Originally published in 1938 by Browne & Nolan,
Clonskeagh, Ireland

© 2019 Reconquista Press
www.reconquistapress.com

ISBN 978-1-912853-07-6

CONTENTS

.../...

.../...

CONTENTS

FOREWORD

As an independent academic, devoted to Irish history for more than 60 years, I've learned that some history is twistory! When events are misrepresented in the popular media of their day to satisfy political patronage and current researchers use that material as source data, they provide a twisted version of history. In researching my latest book: *The Road to a Republic*, I had occasion to focus on Eoin O'Duffy and his contributions to Ireland. I was puzzled at the accounts that denounced him as a fascist and at odds with the Irish Free State. I had known a different Eoin O'Duffy.

From his efforts to defuse the Four Courts debacle that led to the Irish Civil War to his service as third in command to Michael Collins and his meritorious service in that conflict, I saw a man of principle. His later service as Commissioner of the new *Garda Síochána* and founding member of the Army Comrades Association to aid Veterans, further attested to his devotion to comrades and country. Obviously, I had to dig deeper.

I found that a challenging task until I located a long out-of-print copy of *Crusade in Spain*. This was O'Duffy's own account of his sojourn into Spain's military and it not only opened my eyes to his rationale but to his commitment to his faith as well. Using this text as a road map, I explored other sources and confirmed that, at the time, many countries were being subverted by international Communism, even Ireland! Like the pieces of a puzzle, the facts combined to complete a picture of an international anti-Catholic movement that rarely made headlines. I knew that Fascism spawned dictators, but before the likes of Hitler and Mussolini gave dictatorship a bad name, Fascism was the enemy of Communism. And if it took the support of Fascism to beat back the Red threat, then the enemy of my enemy is my ally; so be it! It was there I met the real Eoin O'Duffy.

When I learned that this exciting publication was being reprinted so that all can read the exploits of a remarkable group of dedicated men, whom twistory had written off as misguided and inconsequential, I was delighted. After exploring the new trails that this narrative led me to, I came back with a new hero. His name was Eoin O'Duffy and he went to Spain!

Michael McCormack
National Historian
Ancient Order of Hibernians in America

*I dedicate this book to all my comrades of the Irish brigade,
with special remembrance of our gallant dead.*

INTRODUCTION

M Y HAND is unused to weaving the words that make literature, and I ask the forbearance of my readers while I try
to tell this story of Franco's Crusade in Spain. The full account
of the war, the gathering and sifting of all the facts, must of
course be left to the historians.

I have addressed myself mainly to Irish readers, and my
story claims to be no more than a plain and simple account of
my experience and observations. Its merits, if any, lie in the fact
that it is told by one who was enabled, by living in Spain during
critical months, to sense and know the past Spain, to thrill to the
spirit of the new Spain, and to presume to forecast the outcome
of the present struggle.

In undertaking the task I have been actuated by two main
motives, the one general and the other particular. My general
motive was my realisation that, with few exceptions, the information given to Ireland on this vital Spanish Crusade has come
from tainted sources; my particular motive was a natural desire
to see justice done to the men who, with the Irish Brigade,
played a brave, though unavoidably brief part in the Crusade.

If I have succeeded, even to some small extent, in making
clear the real issue being fought in Spain, and in offering tribute
to the volunteers of the Irish Brigade, then I shall consider as
well repaid the labour I have had in writing this book.

I have to acknowledge my great indebtedness to those
authors from different countries whose works I have cited, to

those newspapers from which I have quoted, and particularly to those who have contributed articles on the Brigade to the *Irish Independent*, from which I got much valuable data. To all I am exceedingly grateful.

Chapter I

LINKS BETWEEN IRELAND AND SPAIN

SPAIN and Ireland have been united through the centuries by the closest bonds of friendship, of faith and of blood. In many parts of Spain today the Irishman is still greeted with the words *Hermano Celta*—Brother Celt—showing he is regarded as of common stock. History shows that our ancestors, the great Milesian warriors, hailed from Spain and for hundreds of years before the birth of Christ had lived there as the rulers of extensive territory.

The traditional account of the Milesians traces them back to the land of Egypt. There it is said this fierce nomadic tribe dwelt in tents by the shores of the Red Sea—their leader, Niall, a powerful eastern prince. Encountering Moses and the Israelites, they treated them with the greatest kindness and hospitality, and for his generosity to the servants of God, Niall was thereupon rewarded by the recovery of his son, Godelius, who lay at the point of death from a snake bite.

Moses promised him that a descendant of his would one day lead his people on a great expedition beyond the seas to inhabit a western isle where no snake or reptile could live.

By this friendship towards the chosen people of God, Niall incurred the wrath of Pharaoh, and was driven forth from his possessions. Thus forced to seek a new country, Niall and his people, after many perilous journeys by land and sea, came into

Spain and were settled there for the greater part of three centuries.

Here, as in Egypt, they tended their flocks and cultivated the land in time of peace, but there were long and bloody wars in which they suffered much at the hands of their neighbours, the savage Goths, whom they finally defeated. Disease and famine then fell upon the land, with most disastrous results. Tired of incessant war, the Milesians once more determined to seek a land where they could live in peace.

A council of the people was held, presided over by the old and feeble warrior Milesius. Calling the Druids, he consulted the ancient books; for they had not forgotten the prophecy given to them by Moses, through their fathers, in the land of Egypt, that one day they would inhabit a far-off western isle. Little was known of that isle save that it lay in the track of the setting sun.

So the first Spanish Armada was fitted out in or about 1000 B.C. It consisted of thirty ships, which carried nine hundred of the best trained warriors and their wives, forming the advance guard of the expedition. Direct from Spain, in the track of a setting sun, our forefathers sailed in search of their promised land—the Emerald Isle of Destiny.

> They came from a land beyond the sea,
>   And now o'er the western main
> Set sail, in their good ships, gallantly,
>   From the sunny land of Spain.
>
> 'Tis Innisfail—'tis Innisfail:
>   Rings o'er the echoing sea;
> While, bending to heav'n, the warriors hail
>   That home of the brave and free.

After a long buffeting by storms and seas the Milesians beached their sturdy galleys in Kerry, and, according to legend, engaged the Tuatha De Dananns on the Sliabh Mis Mountain. They defeated the De Dananns amid great slaughter and not before their brave Queen Scota, widow of Milesius, had fallen mortally wounded.

Having buried her with all the honours of war and, after their custom, upright in her grave, with her face to the rising sun, they pushed on northwards, and at Tailteann fought the final battle which made them masters of the country. Ireland, which they called Scota, to honour their dead Queen, was divided between the twin sons of Milesius, Heber and Heremon. Later a dispute arose between the two brothers as to who should be the ruler of all Ireland. In the battle that followed, at Geashill, Heber was slain, and Heremon was crowned Ard Rí—King of Ireland.

Thus was the dynasty founded which gave Ireland Ollamh Fodla, who established the Feis of Tara, Conn of the Hundred Battles, Cormac Mac Art, Niall of the Nine Hostages, Dathi, Laoghaire, Malachi, Brian Boru, and Roderick O'Conor, the last Ard Rí of Ireland.

From these ancient times onward there was a constant traffic between the two countries, and few ports in Munster and the West have not seen the tall Spanish merchantmen.

In the Middle Ages, when Ireland's scholars had world renown, students from all parts of Spain received the hospitality of the Irish universities, and Irish monks taught in the monasteries of Castile. Moreover, the Spaniards came to regard Ireland as a place of sanctity and pilgrimage, and many of them crossed the seas, braving all the perils of the journey, disagreeable as it must have been in those days, in order to visit the cave of St. Patrick in Lough Derg, which they regarded as the gate to Heaven. They looked on Ireland as a land rich in the fruits of the earth, where men lived lives of sanctity and occupied themselves in the pursuits of learning and art. Here, too, the climate was mild and the land yielded an hundredfold to the husbandman.

Similarly Irish pilgrims journeyed to the shrine of St. James the Apostle at Compostela, in West Galicia. "Over in Galicia," writes Dr. Walter Starkie, "every Irishman comes into his own, and in the evening in the towns he will hear the sounds of the

Irish bagpipes to fill him with homesickness for the 'Rakes of Mallow', the 'Kinnegad Slashers' and the 'Antrim Lasses'. When he goes to pray in Santiago Cathedral he will see the tomb of Thomas, Archbishop of Cashel, who died there in 1654."

Here, the city of Galway probably shows most strongly the influence of former days when it carried on a flourishing trade with Spain, exporting hides and wool for Spanish silks and wines. Many of Galway's architectural gems owe their existence to the wealthy Spanish merchants who settled there. The dark-eyed Galway colleen, hiding her beauty beneath that coloured shawl, and the tall dark fisher lad from the Claddagh are as Spanish as any Spaniard I met in my journeying through Spain. The story of the Spartan justice of Lynch, who hanged his own son, found guilty of the murder of a young Spaniard who crossed him in love, is well known.

Columbus, the great explorer, on his way in search of the new world called at the port of Galway, it is said, attended Mass in the Cathedral St. Nicholas of Myra, and took a number of Galway seafaring men with him. Amongst them, the story runs, was one O'Flaherty, who was the first to sight America.

When the glories of the Middle Ages had given way to the long penal night, Spain helped Ireland with a generosity we should at all times remember. During the years of persecution, when the penal code of our English rulers almost extinguished the lamps of Irish learning and religion, many thousands of students were welcomed and educated in the universities of Spain. Between the thirteenth and seventeenth centuries the numbers of Irish students in Spain were so great that it was found impossible to receive them all into Spanish seminaries and the College of Salamanca was "built by the Kingdom of Castile for the support of the Catholic religion in Ireland". King Philip, in a letter to the Rector of the University at Salamanca, wrote concerning the Irish students: "Favour and aid them, for they have left their own country, and all they possessed in it in the service of God our Lord, and for the preservation of the Catholic Faith." In

Madrid arose Spain's generous gift to our exiled students of the seventeenth century, the beautiful *"La Iglesia de la Irlandeses."*

How important was the training given the students is recorded in the Annals of the Irish Dominicans. "These young men came from Spain," it is written, "not only thoroughly educated in the principles of the religious life, learnt in the country of St. Dominic and St. Teresa, but also with a touch of Spanish chivalric devotion to the Catholic Faith, which seemed to animate them all with a bold and fearless spirit."

How the British Government looked upon Ireland's connections with Spain during those days is best gleaned from the State Papers. Evidently it caused not a little anxiety, for we read: "The priests land here secretly in every port and creek of the realm, and afterwards disperse themselves into several quarters in such sorts that every town and county is full of them. And the most alarming thing of all is they are everywhere undoing the work of the reformer."

I cannot deal here at any length on the glorious achievements of the Irish Brigades in the service of Spain, and can only commend the young student of history to go further afield in the realms of research. The State Papers throw much light on the high positions attained, and the esteem and favour in which Irishmen were held by Philip.

During the long struggle of the O'Neills and O'Donnells with the British invader Ireland was in close touch with Spain. O'Neill encouraged his men to enter the service of Spain to learn the art of war. They studied under the best military authorities of the day. His own son was received by Philip and educated in the Spanish Military Academy in Madrid. He returned to Ireland bearing a letter from the King, promising aid and munitions for the Irish cause. The hospitality shown by Hugh O'Neill to the survivors of the Spanish Armada, wrecked off Ireland in 1591, soon drew upon him the suspicion of Britain. Whisperings of Irish plots and intrigue with Spain became rampant in Dublin and London.

In September, 1601, the promised Spanish help arrived off Kinsale, but, unhappily, on account of the distance from Ulster, it was of little use to the Irish chieftains. Some historians even go so far as to say that it ruined the Irish cause, but here I am concerned only with the goodwill that prompted the Spanish monarch and his people to send us aid. Had the commander of the expedition, Don Juan d'Aguila, landed in the North, according to plan, there is a high probability that the Irish cause would have triumphed then.

An earlier landing of eight hundred Spanish troops in Smerwick Harbour, Co. Kerry, failed for similar reasons. The south of Ireland was completely disorganised at the time, and after the Spanish were disarmed they were massacred at Dunanore by the British forces in most brutal fashion.

After the battle of Kinsale, O'Donnell went to Spain to explain personally to King Philip, on behalf of O'Neill and himself, the cause of the failure. He was received by the King with all the honours due to a member of a royal family. While engaged in negotiating for another Spanish expedition to aid the Catholic cause in Ireland, O'Donnell was poisoned by a hired assassin of Britain—a renegade Irishman named Blake. In 1602 he was buried in Valladolid, and it was there my offer of Irish aid was accepted by the late General Mola on behalf of General Franco, on 28th September, 1936. "Red Hugh's memory lives on in Spain," testifies our Dr. Starkie, "and many a vagabond in Spain has heard 'O'Donnell Abu' on pipes or fiddle."

Those who welcomed the new Irish Brigade included the present direct representative of the House of the O'Donnells— the Duchess of Tetuan. Of most charming manner, she retains that simple yet queenly dignity which once graced the royal halls of Tyrconnell. She has a deep affection for the home of her forefathers, and in the event of the re-establishment of the old Kingdom of Ireland would really appear to have a prior claim. She showed the keenest practical interest in the Brigade, and offered that should we succeed in bringing out further contingents she would travel to the United States to raise funds in our aid. She is a direct descendant of the last Irishman to attain to high power in Spain—Leopold O'Donnell, who became Premier in 1858. His five years in office were among the most prosperous in that country's history.

When the Irish chiefs and followers fled from their unhappy land Ireland was for long consoled by the valour and chivalry of her exiles. If we have since forgotten them, it is not so in Spain. They are remembered well. Today young Spaniards recall many tales of daring of the Irishmen who fought under Spain's banner long ago.

The men of the Irish Brigade of today had, indeed, a great historic background. They went to repay in some slight measure the vast debt that their forefathers owed to their fellow Christians of Spain.

> *Remember us when you arise again,*
> *Remember us when you return to reign,*
> *Oh, Christ-like nation, martyred, splendid Spain!*
> (Aodh de Blácam)

SPAIN'S APPEAL TO IRELAND — THE RESPONSE — FRANCO ACCEPTS OUR OFFER — THE ALCÁZAR EPIC

"IRELAND is behind the people of Spain in their fight for the Faith. Irish volunteers are making ready to leave home to fight side by side with the Nationalist forces, convinced that the cause of Franco is the cause of Christian civilisation." That, in brief, was the message I brought the late General Mola on 23rd September, 1936.

Of the events which had so deeply stirred the heart of Ireland, and produced the support which I was thus able to offer Franco I write fully in a later chapter. The appeal from Spain to Ireland and the answer form my subject now.

I was about to leave Dublin for a short holiday with some friends at The Hague, when I received an appeal from a Spaniard in London—prominent in the Carlist movement. "My country," he wrote, "is in the thrall of a most terrific death struggle, trying to free itself from the horrible and vile Communist and Marxist rule and the ghastly influence of Soviet Russia. Unquestionably it is going to be a hard fight for us, and obviously of the most vital importance to the whole Christian world.

"If we lose, God help us. Our poor, already suffering, country will be utterly broken and degraded, and reduced to a loathsome dependency of Soviet Russia with an anti-Christ

Government. Surely the Christian countries of Europe could not possibly look with favour upon the prospects of Spain as a new outpost of Russia.

"Apparently poor France has been tricked into an alliance with her, and there is absolutely no doubt that the strong Soviet influences prevailing in the present French Government will do all in their power to help our enemies, notwithstanding what so-called agreements may be come to with other Powers regarding our situation.

"Do you think it might be possible to raise in Ireland a volunteer force to come to aid us—purely personally voluntary, so as to avoid all possibility of international complications? What a glorious example Ireland could give the whole of Christendom!

"This heroic movement in Spain was really started by the party to which I have the honour to belong—the Carlist-Traditionalists, essentially the most Catholic movement in Spain, whose headquarters have ever been in Pamplona, the capital of Navarra, the home of the Carlist movement. The Carlists, other parties of the 'Right' and the Army—all have joined together and come to an agreement to submerge all political aspirations and unite on the one vital point—which is the ridding our beloved country of the pestilential canker of Communism and the influence of Soviet Russia.

"We Carlists have up to now placed in the field 30,000 well armed men, and we hope to raise as many more. If your brave, noble Irish came to our help they should be placed in the Carlist command. In any case, please, I beg of you to pardon the liberty I am taking in addressing you on behalf of my country."

The idea of an Irish Brigade for Spain had not entered my mind until then, but this letter set me thinking. I knew that the sympathy of Ireland was on the side of those fighting against the enemies of our Church, but sympathy was not enough now. A call for men had come. What was I to do?

I discussed the matter with a few friends, but they discouraged me, saying that with my limited resources the project, however meritorious, was impossible of achievement.

I acknowledged the letter briefly, promising to write as soon as I was in a position to give a definite reply. Then, leaving for Holland, I wrote to the Dublin papers, suggesting the formation of an Irish Volunteer Brigade for service in Spain, and giving possible volunteers time to think it over. Realising the grave responsibility attached to such a venture I did not appeal then, or at any time subsequently, for volunteers. I merely stated the issue at stake as it appeared to me—that General Franco was holding the trenches, not only for Spain, but for Christianity. I fully recognised that it was unlikely that any number of men we could send to Spain would be of great military assistance. On the other hand, the very fact that a group of Irishmen volunteered their services in the Christian cause could not fail to have a good moral effect, and favourable reactions elsewhere.

On my return to Dublin from Holland, I learned that various public bodies had passed resolutions calling on the Government to break off diplomatic relations and to cease trading with Red Spain. Generally, the volume of protest raised all over the country against the Communists in Spain, by people holding diverse political views, was very encouraging. On a few platforms, of course, and at meetings of a few public bodies politicians attributed ulterior motives to me.

Every post now brought me hundreds of letters from all over Ireland and from Irishmen in Britain and other countries offering their services for a volunteer brigade. By the time it was announced that no further applications could be considered over six thousand had volunteered. The final announcement had only the effect of increasing the post each morning, while young men from Dublin and the neighbouring counties called on me in large numbers.

The applications, be it said, were not so much from youths fired with the spirit of adventure, or lured by the glamour of soldiers marching to battle, as from responsible citizens in every phase of Irish life—farmers' sons, industrial workers, trades-men, teachers, soldiers, civic guards. True, we had youths in the ranks—more than a hundred of those who travelled to Spain were under twenty-one years of age, and over a thousand youths made application altogether. There were also many such volun-teers as Major O'Malley, Suir Castle, Co. Tipperary (Knight of Malta); and Lt.-Col. P. R. Butler, son of the late General Sir William Butler.

The response was so prompt, so generous and so spontane-ous, that I could only regard it as a mandate to go ahead with the organisation of the brigade. I decided to do so. Communi-cating with my Carlist friend, I informed him of the position and a meeting in London was arranged. On meeting him, inci-dentally, I enquired why he wrote to me in particular, and was informed that my name was given to him by a distinguished Irish ecclesiastic to whom he wrote in the first instance.

Having discussed the project at some length, we deemed it advisable to place the proposals before Franco's general head-quarters. I prepared a memorandum on conditions of service, uniforms, numbers, transport, routes, international complica-tions, and so on. This was sent by special courier to Spain, and on 20th September the same courier arrived in Dublin with a reply signifying general agreement, but necessitating a personal interview with the higher command. Next morning I left Dublin by plane on the long journey to Valladolid, *via* London, Paris, St. Jean de Luz, Pamplona, and Burgos.

When I crossed the International bridge into Spain, a guard of honour presented arms. I was received by two members of the Government of Navarra and left immediately with a mili-tary escort for Pamplona, the capital of Navarra and Carlist headquarters. On the way we halted at the Capuchin monastery at Elizondo, where we were entertained by the Guardian, Father Augustine. Many of the Fathers recalled visits to Roch-estown in Co. Cork, to Dublin and Kilkenny. They wept with joy on hearing that Ireland wished to help the cause of the Faith in Spain. The college had been converted into an hospital for wounded Carlist soldiers—victors of Irun and San Sebastián.

After visiting the wards and seeing the sacred relics I left with my party on the journey across the Pyrenees, for Pamplona. At the door of the palace of the Deputación—the seat of the Government of Navarra—I was met by the President, Don Juan Pedro Arraiza, and conducted to the throne room to be greeted by the Provincial Government and the Carlist High Command.

I stayed overnight at the palace, and in the morning, after attending Mass in the palace chapel with the President and War Council, left for Burgos. The Acting President of Franco's new National Government, General Cabanellas, informed me there that General Mola was awaiting me at his headquarters at Valladolid. I reached there shortly after dark, and was at once brought to the General's room to be received most cordially.

We talked for an hour, the General referring to the historic bonds between Ireland and Spain, to the O'Donnells, the O'Neills, and other great Irish families who had become part of the Spanish nation.

General Mola was in charge of the entire army north of and including Madrid, and while I was talking with him couriers arrived with messages from the various fronts. Nevertheless he spoke with me as if mine was the only business he had to do. He then went on to talk of Toledo, and tears came into his eyes as he spoke of the gallant cadets who had been holding out in the Alcázar for ten weeks. "Please God, we will soon relieve them," he said. He was outlining for me on a map the position of the Nationalist Army there when his Chief of Staff entered the room, saluted and said "Generalissimo, Señor."

General Mola lifted the telephone receiver. General Franco was speaking. They exchanged but a few words, then General Mola, laying down the receiver, exclaimed "Alcázar." He rushed towards me and embraced me in an ecstasy of joy. His voice was heard in the ante-room, and his officers rushed in to congratulate him and share his delight. In a few minutes a huge crowd had assembled in the Plaza outside headquarters and

General Mola appeared on the balcony. It was several minutes before he could make himself heard through the cheering. Then he announced officially that Toledo had fallen, that the heroes of the Alcázar were liberated. There was no peace in Valladolid that night, or indeed next day, for the public rejoicing began immediately. And how the Spanish can celebrate!

The epic of the Alcázar was such however as to justify even the most extraordinary joy, to inspire everyone who hears of it with a new belief in the heroic strength of human nature, to show how vital were the principles for which the Alcázar defenders fought, and for which their comrades-in-arms still fight.

On another visit to Spain I attended a Requiem Mass which was celebrated in the ruins for the souls of its dead defenders. After the Mass a captain of the garrison acted as my guide and detailed for me the story of the siege and of the desperate resistance. The moving account took on an added solemnity from the simple modest telling, there amid the ruins, by one of the band whom death, in its most terrible forms—by famine, dynamite, poison gas, and liquid fire—had assailed for two long months and failed to conquer. "It was Our Lady," said the captain simply as he bade us farewell. I thought then of the new shrine I had seen in Toledo Cathedral, which is crowded all day with worshippers. A little statue of Our Lady is now enthroned there—the statue of Our Lady of the Alcázar. Around this statue the devotion of the faithful garrison had centred during the long siege, and now all Catholic Spain reveres with them Our Lady of the Alcázar.

Here is a translation of the official summary of the Alcázar record, which I obtained from General Franco's office:

Days of siege: 70. From 21st July to 28th September, 1936.
Guns in action against the Alcázar:

15·5	9
10·5	4
7·5	7

Rounds fired: 15·5 guns   3,300
                      10·5   "   3,000
                       7·5   "   3,500
                  50 mm. mortar   2,000

Total number of shells fired into the Alcázar   11,800
Number of hand grenades fired   1,500
Dynamite bombs   2,000
Attempts at assault   8
Attacks by aviation   30
Bombs dropped by aviation   500
Petrol tanks by aviation   35
Inflammable liquid in bottles   200
Fires produced by aeroplane attacks   10
Big mines fired   2
Smaller mines fired   2
Maximum number of 15·5 shells fired in one day   472
Combatants in the Alcázar   1,100
Of these killed   82
Of these wounded seriously   430
Of these wounded slightly   150
Of those disappeared after explosions   57
Unaccounted for, or deserters   30
Died natural deaths   5
Suicides   3
Total casualties   59%
Officers killed   23%
Officers wounded   14%
Women inside Alcázar   520
Children inside Alcázar   50
Casualties among women and children   Nil
Natural deaths among women and children   2
                                   (over 70 years old)
Births   2
                                  (1 boy and 1 girl)
Horses inside Alcázar   97
Mules inside Alcázar   27

When Alcázar relieved .... 1 horse and 5 mules still alive
                                    The horse is a famous
                                    prize-winning jumper.
Outbreak of disease .... Nil
Water .... Allowance 1 litre per day.
                        No washing—personal or clothing.

Although the story of the heroism of Colonel Moscardo, the commander of the Alcázar garrison, has been widely told, I think it is appropriate to include it here.

He was a Director at the Military Academy at Toledo and, early in July, 1936, had gone to Madrid to prepare for the departure of a body of cadets to attend the Olympic Games in Berlin. When, upon the murder of Calvo Sotelo, the political atmosphere thickened, Colonel Moscardo considered it wiser to return to his post without delay. He installed himself first in the house of the Military Governor and then moved to the Alcázar with one thousand three hundred armed men and civilians and five hundred women and children fleeing from the Red terror.

Colonel Moscardo had been too busy ordering and arranging the retreat to think of his own family. In the Alcázar he found that his wife and two youngest children had been left outside in the hands of the mob. He kept this news and his terrible grief to himself; for, above all other considerations, was that of military duty. It was not the time for useless lament or depressing news, he decided nobly, but an hour for accepting any sacrifice, however great, for the welfare of his country.

So he set about organising the defence, arranging for the victualling and munitioning of the force under his command. On the first day of the siege, too, he began the diary of the campaign, which the regulations of the Spanish army require of every commander of a besieged fortress.

That diary was not to be interrupted on any day, not even on the terrible day of St. James the Apostle, Patron of Spain, when the world seemed to be tumbling about their heads, nor on the dread day when Azaña, President of the Republic, and Largo

Caballero, Prime Minister, looked on from a distance at the blowing up of the Alcázar. The sun was darkened that day with the cloud of rock and stone that was thrown to a long distance from Toledo.

Colonel Moscardo's magnificent sense of duty led him even to sacrifice his own son. Curious circumstance, a telephone wire still connected the Alcázar with the outside world, and on July 24th Colonel Moscardo was rung up and called upon to surrender the Alcázar.

"If you do not do so," the Red officer in command said, "I will have your son shot, whom I hold prisoner by my side."

"Neither the life of my son nor the lives of my whole family could make me swerve from the path of duty. Military honour is superior to threats," replied Moscardo.

"We shall see. Your son shall speak to you now."

The voice of Luis Moscardo, seventeen years of age, then came over the wire to his father.

"Hullo, father!"

"What is it, boy?"

"Only that they are going to shoot me if you don't surrender."

"My dearest boy, you know how I feel. If they are going to shoot you, you had better commend your soul to God, give a *Viva!* for Spain, and die like a hero; for your father, for the honour of Spain, will not surrender."

"That's right, father."

"Goodbye, boy! Be brave!"

And Luis Moscardo did meet his death bravely when executed three weeks later, a couple of hundred yards away from the Alcázar.

At last, on a brilliant morning in September, when the sunshine was reflected on the bayonets of the relieving force, Colonel Moscardo stumbled out of the ruins of the fortress, followed by a procession of spectres. Slowly approaching the General in command of the relief column, General Varela, he came to attention and saluted, saying: "Nothing to report from the Alcázar, sir."

General Mola came back to his office and we resumed our talk. He was enthusiastic about the Irish Brigade, and we discussed the scheme. The final decision rested, of course, with General Franco himself, and General Mola said he would travel by plane next morning to confer with the Generalissimo at general headquarters in Cáceres. As he had afterwards to go from Cáceres to Pamplona to attend the funeral of a General who had been killed in action a few days previously, he bade me an affectionate goodbye. I never saw him again, for he was afterwards killed during another of his dashes by air.

The result of his conference at general headquarters was conveyed to me by his Chief of Staff, who flew back to Valladolid. It was brief—"General Franco gladly accepts Ireland's offer of a volunteer brigade." The decision was made public through the loud speakers while Valladolid was celebrating the Alcázar victory, and there was cheer after cheer for Ireland. As the massed troops and crowds sang the Felange Hymn during the evening, *Viva Irlande* was substituted for *Viva España*.

That night I broadcast a message from military headquarters at Valladolid, by request. "As a Catholic and an Irishman," I said at the microphone, "I came here a few days ago to visit Patriot territory with strong sympathies for the Patriot cause. But I never felt I could be so carried away with enthusiasm as I have been. I see the spirit of a great and historic nation standing like tested steel to preserve again, as Spain so often preserved in the past, the glory of Christian civilisation against the onslaughts of a heathen foe. Ireland can never forget that when she was in agony in a similar struggle, Spain was her only ally and friend in all the world.

"For my part—and I think I speak for many Irishmen in every part of the world—Ireland will leave nothing undone to help her historic friend and ally in the glorious crusade which is now being carried on so successfully here."

Chapter III

NON-INTERVENTION LAW IN IRELAND —
FREE STATE GOVERNMENT'S ATTITUDE —
IRISHMEN ON THE RED FRONT

O N MY RETURN to Ireland within a couple of days, I found non-intervention and its possible effect on the Irish brigade the subject of great conjecture.

The *Irish Times* had discussed the matter with "a well-known constitutional lawyer", who gave it as his opinion that my action constituted a criminal offence. Others held that the Non-Intervention Pact, to which the Free State had become a party, enabled the Government to act.

"A Lawyer," writing in the *Irish Independent*, said: "The Foreign Enlistment Act of 1870 refers to British subjects only, and after the passing of the Citizenship Act of 1935 by the Dáil, no citizen of Saorstát Eireann is any longer a British subject. In regard to the Non-Intervention Pact, the terms of this agreement with other Powers by the Free State have no legal force here until ratified by an Act of the Oireachtas."

Evidently the Government accepted the last-mentioned view, for some time later the Spanish Civil War (Non-Intervention) Bill was introduced and hurriedly passed through the Dáil. To participate in the Spanish war was made an offence punishable by a fine not exceeding £500, or at the discretion of the Court imprisonment for a term not exceeding two years, or by both such fine and imprisonment. It was also enacted that no citizen might leave the Free State for the purpose of proceeding to Spain without a special endorsement on his passport, and the issue of a ticket for such purposes was made an offence.

The conflict in Spain has been referred to as the Spanish Civil War. This is entirely misleading and tends to minimise the enormity of the task which General Franco undertook in the fight against the spread of Communism in Western Europe. We have heard the Nationalist troops referred to as rebels, while the Reds are referred to as Government forces. Others still refer to the war as a fight between two "isms". To quote the Marquis Merry del Val: "We might as well say of the judge who sentences a criminal to death, 'they are six of one and half a dozen of the other'."

Portugal, for instance, refused to enter into diplomatic relations with Soviet Russia, or even to admit a trade representative from that country. She did not recognise the Red Government, and refused to enter into diplomatic or trade relations with it. When requested to prohibit the transport of arms to General Franco through Portugal, she replied that she was prepared and willing to do so provided other countries ceased sending supplies to the Communists. Like Ireland, Portugal is a Catholic country. She is under greater obligation to Britain than we are, but she is determined, and she wants the world to know it, that Communism will never be allowed to raise its head there.

There are perhaps sound imperial reasons for Britain to fear a Franco victory, but why should the Free State share those fears? General Franco told me he was very disappointed and surprised at the attitude of a country with the Catholic tradition of Ireland. He would have prized highly the recognition of our Government some time ago. A lead from Ireland then would have meant much to the cause. Merely following recognition by England it could be of little value.

The Irish Free State was represented in Madrid by an Envoy Extraordinary and Minister Plenipotentiary. While I am aware that the Minister visited Burgos and Salamanca and interested himself in the repatriation of minors in the Irish brigade, the fact remains that he is accredited to the Red Government and is thus officially a member of their Diplomatic Corps.

The Spanish Minister in Dublin, Señor d'Aguilar, resigned in September, 1936, on the grounds that "the Government he represented here did not represent the Spanish nation. The Government," he said, "is simply a screen behind which the Anarchist and Communist Committees control. The Cabinet Ministers are prisoners of these Committees." This is the opinion of one who ought to know, expressed by him in the Irish newspapers as far back as September, 1936. When the Spanish Minister resigned because his Government did not represent Spain a splendid opportunity presented itself to the Free State Government to withdraw the Irish Minister from Red Spain. But no action was taken.

There were interesting references to the Free State's position made in the British House of Commons and in the English newspapers. Mr. Manders, M.P., asked the Home Secretary why action was not taken "to prevent British ports being used by General O'Duffy for the transport of the Irish Brigade to Spain", and Mr. Roberts, M.P., asked "On what date he learned that there was being organised by General O'Duffy in the Irish Free State an expedition to fight against the Spanish Government, and what steps he took to prevent this expedition, or any men in it using British ports as a base for the departure for Spain, and in particular what steps were taken to prevent General O'Duffy and his adherents sailing from Liverpool, and whether the Dominions Secretary made representations to the Saorstát Government that their obligations as signatories to the Covenant of the League of Nations are inconsistent with allowing such an expedition to be organised, and that the Foreign Enlistment Act applies equally to the Saorstát."

Mr. Malcolm MacDonald said that he was aware that a number of Irish Free State citizens left that country towards the end of last year with the object of enlisting in the forces of General Franco. The question of prohibiting the recruitment and departure of volunteers for Spain was recently referred by the Non-Intervention Committee to the Governments concerned. He understood that the replies of the various Governments, including that of the Irish Free State, were now before the Committee.

Sir John Simon said, "Before proceedings could be taken it is necessary that evidence should be available to satisfy the Court that an offence has in fact been committed, and after evidence has been collected it would be necessary to show that the accused is within the jurisdiction of the Court. My information is that these conditions are not satisfied in General O'Duffy's case."

Professor Keith, Edinburgh, an authority on constitutional law, in a letter to the English newspapers wrote: "It is clear that shipping British subjects from the United Kingdom is an illegality which there is abundant provision to prevent. Why, therefore, has not this power been used to prevent General O'Duffy using the port of Liverpool for the transport of his Irish Brigade, or has Mr. Eden's sincerity in the doctrine of non-intervention suffered qualification from a desire to avoid interference with General O'Duffy? The fact that the Irish Free State Government does not enforce the Act of 1870 is easily explained by the religion of the people, but this affords no justification for the deliberate omission of the British Government to prevent the use of British ports for purposes hostile to a friendly Government. Moreover, the Free State is a party to the Non-Intervention agreement. Is it proposed to ask Mr. de Valera to put into operation the Act? Or is it intended that while Germany, Italy and Russia should be pressed to prevent volunteering for one side or the other, the Free State alone should be free to send aid to the insurgent cause? The Free State, it may be remembered, has not recognised the insurgents as the legitimate Government of Spain or even as belligerents."

There was another reference in the British Commons.

Mr. Gallacher (Communist) said: "The Bill is deliberately designed to keep arms away from the Spanish Government. We are told there is no proof of arms passing through Portugal, but we have General O'Duffy's brigade proceeding through Liverpool, not to America or North Africa, but to Lisbon."

Mr. Runciman (for the Government) replied: "The Dominions have been informed of our proposal, but we have not yet had any indication from them as to their attitude on it. It is entirely a matter for the Dominions themselves. Only the Irish Free State is a party to the Non-Intervention European agreement. It is a remarkable fact."

On the Red front Ireland has been represented by a small group—a few from Dublin and Belfast, but mostly men of Irish descent from Britain and U.S.A., making "a gesture of the sympathy of the revolutionary Ireland with the Spanish people".

Captain C. J. McGuinness, an Irishman who fought with this group for a while, has described his experiences. "We were marched into our barracks in Albacete, and once inside I realised that I was in the chapel of a religious building—a monastery or convent. A large statue of Our Lord lay broken in the *patio*—altar candelabra were strewn everywhere. Later I learned that forty priests and nuns had been executed here a week previous. Sleeping quarters were provided in the violated chapel, but, loath to sleep there, I found a small nook on the top floor.

"When I came down in the morning I found the troops exploring the place and having a rare orgy of blasphemy. Some were marching round the church attired in sacred vestments. A group of Jew boys were swinging incense burners. On the altar another group was mimicking the Mass. Up in the organ gallery a Frenchman was playing the *Internationale* in slow time, and all were chanting an accompaniment. In the niches in the chapel walls stood Hebrew legionaries in clerical robes. The displaced statues lay broken on the floor beneath. A depraved looking Slav was breaking the cover of the Mass book, laughing like an idiot. Latrines were erected in the square—wooden tubs, draped with altar cloths and vestments. . . .

"We got orders to move to Madrid. The section of the road we were travelling was well known to be hot. At any moment we might be ambushed. Then I would possibly have to fight in a cause for which I had lost all sympathy. . . ."

Captain McGuinness has described also his experiences in the fighting line and how later he succeeded in getting across the frontier into France. He concludes:

"The Madrid Government is one hundred per cent Red and violently opposed to the Catholic Church. Any Irishman fighting for or defending this regime is defending the enemy of his Faith. I learned these facts by bitter experience."

More serious than the presence of a group of Irishmen on the Red front was a cablegram sent from a congress in Dublin to Largo Caballero, then Red Premier of Spain, assuring him of Ireland's sympathy and support. Speaking in Drogheda, shortly afterwards, His Eminence Cardinal MacRory said: "It is a scandal and an outrage for an Irish Catholic body to send publicly a promise of support to the Communist leader of a movement that seeks to destroy faith in God, and faith in the world to come, and that is pledged to destroy every Christian State in the world if it can. It is a very serious matter, and in my opinion one for the State to take notice of. Whatever the State may do it is our duty to pray for Spain, and for those poor misguided sons of Ireland."

Chapter IV

THE HOLIEST WAR — THE CHURCH'S VIEW

ONE APRIL MORNING Jerusalem awakened to the shouts of a half-demented mob gathered outside the house of Pilate clamouring for the Blood of Him Who they said was perverting their nation. And Pilate, while knowing he was not justified, yielded in his weakness to the demands of the crowd and delivered Jesus to them to be put to death. Nearly two thousand years later a similar scene took place outside the seat of Government in Madrid. A howling rabble demanded the blood of the priests of Spain because they, too, were perverting the nation. The Government, like Pilate, yielded to the demand of the mob and delivered the priests to them to suffer like their Master the tortures and pains of Calvary, including, in many cases, actual crucifixion. Men, as if possessed of all the characteristics of the beast, sunk to the lowest depths of human passion and degradation, cried out once more for the blood of Christ and His priests, "Away with Him, crucify Him. His blood be upon us and our children."

We read in the Joint Letter signed by forty-three Cardinals, Archbishops and Bishops of Spain addressed to the Bishops of the world: "'I had sworn to be revenged on You' said one of them to Our Lord enclosed in the tabernacle, and aiming at Him with a pistol, he fired on Him saying: 'Surrender to the Reds! Surrender to Marxism!'" The war on Christianity had begun.

41

His Eminence Cardinal Hayes, Archbishop of New York, spoke thus of the Spanish tragedy: "Let us turn our eyes in tears towards Spain. There arises in vision before me a noble monument of Christ in a public square in Spain, erected there years ago to express the love of His heart for mankind; a statue representing gentleness, kindness and mercy. How horrible it is to think that men should have gone so bad as to have a firing squad actually assault His sacred head. True it is He can no longer endure suffering or death itself. But He suffers in the members of His mystical Body, those courageous martyrs, bishops, priests, nuns and faithful, who have met violent deaths from the diabolical blood-crazed enemies of God and of His Church."

And here is the summing up of the Leftist leader Lerroux, one of the outstanding figures in Spanish politics, and several times Republican Premier after the fall of the monarchy:

"General Franco's revolt is not a military rising against the law, but for the law, not against the people, but for the safety of the people. It is a national rising as legitimate and holy as the war of Independence in 1808. It is even more sacred, for it is not only a question of political independence, but of home, property, culture, conscience and very life—in a word our whole civilisation as handed down in history. When the army took up arms the people, without distinction of class or outlook, deliberately took their stand by the side of the army, and shed their blood in common with the army from the very first day."

It was certainly not a Fascist rising against the "lawfully elected Government", and neither was it an attempt by the command of the Spanish army to set up a military dictatorship. These charges have been printed in foreign newspapers, who insist that all the Right Wing movement in Spain is Fascist. The truth is that the Fascist movement in Spain prior to the revolt was of little or no importance. In the elections of 1933 their strength in the Cortes was negligible, and in the general election of 1936 they did not secure a single seat. Franco is not a Fascist, Mola was not a Fascist, none of the Nationalist leaders are Fascist.

The revolt, as the Spanish Hierarchy pointed out, was a civic-military rising, an armed plebiscite of the Spanish people.

In order legitimately to claim the obedience of its citizens a Government must first be elected by the majority of the people entitled to vote. When so elected it has certain defined duties to carry out, such as the protection of life and property. It must not violate such rights of the citizens as the free exercise of religion, and the right to hold property. Laws passed contrary to these fundamental rights have no moral binding force whatsoever, and the people are bound to resist them even to the extent of armed revolt. This is the only case where the Catholic Church permits physical force. All the elements necessary for lawful insurrection were present in the case of Franco's Nationalist revolt. It was therefore morally lawful.

"On the side of the insurgents," say the Hierarchy of Spain, "the defence of order, social, peace, traditional civilisation, mother country, and very markedly the defence of religion; on the other—materialism, be it called Marxist, Communist or Anarchist, which wants to substitute for the old civilisation of Spain the ultra-new 'civilisation' of the Russian Soviets. On the one side God is suppressed, on the other the old spirit—Christian and Spanish—is preserved. There is no hope in Spain for the reconquering of justice and peace and the blessings that derive from them other than the triumph of the Nationalist movement."

The Church approved of the Nationalist revolt and hailed General Franco as the deliverer of his people, but it never encouraged war as a means to national salvation. The charge of belligerency made against the Church by many foreign newspapers is as unfounded as it is absurd. "The Church," write the Spanish Hierarchy, "has neither wished for this war nor provoked it. She has given the highest example of apostolic and civic moderation. Whoever accuses the Church of having provoked this war, or even of not having done all that in her lay to avoid it, does not know, or falsifies the reality. The Church was persecuted before the war broke out, and since then she has been the chief victim of the fury of one of the contending parties, which aimed openly and directly at the abolition of the Catholic Church in Spain. We Spanish Bishops could not remain silent without abandoning the interests of Christ."

The Irish Hierarchy in their reply to the letter of the Spanish Hierarchy, say: "The world Press, with some honourable exceptions, has grievously misled the nations on the origin of the Spanish civil war, on the principles involved, and on the issues at stake in that momentous conflict."

In England the Catholic Church, on the feast of St. James the Apostle, Patron of Spain, prayed for the victory of the Nationalist forces, and for peace in the distracted land of Spain.

The Most Rev. Richard Fitzgerald, Bishop of Gibraltar (native of Midleton, Co. Cork) says: "The future of religion, of order, and of well-being is at stake, not only in Spain, but in a great part of the world."

His Eminence Cardinal MacRory, speaking at Drogheda, as far back as September, 1936, said: "Poor Spain! So long a great country and a faithful friend of Ireland, now torn and bleeding and fighting for her Christian life. There is no room any longer for any doubt as to the issues at stake in the Spanish conflict. It is not a question of the army against the people, nor of the aristocracy plus the army and the Church against labour. Not at all. It is a question of whether Spain will remain as she has been so long, a Christian and Catholic land, or a Bolshevist and anti-God land."

The authoritative teachers spoke clearly and definitely. The Holy Father, profoundly touched by such atrocities, called on the whole of Christendom to pray for the speedy victory of the Spanish nation over the powers of darkness. Addressing Spanish refugees, in September, 1936, His Holiness said: "Our Benediction, above any political or mundane consideration, goes out in an especial manner to all those who have assumed the difficult and dangerous task of defending and restoring the rights and honour of God and religion."

Our Lord, in the presence of the soldiers who had put upon Him the agonies of the Cross, cried: "Father forgive them, for they know not what they do." His words have had many an echo from the Spanish cities and towns where His ministers have been martyred. No more marvellous instance of this Christ-like spirit could be given, perhaps, than that told me by Arnold Lunn, the writer, whom I met in Seville during Holy Week.

"A priest," he said, "was being led out to his death. He was bound, and as he faced his executioners he said: 'I want to bless you. Please free my hands.' A Red cut the ropes and hacked off the priest's hands. 'Bless us now', he sneered, and the priest, raising his bleeding stumps, did bless them before he died."

On the one hand, therefore, was the great leader and patriot, General Franco, at the head of the Nationalist movement, composed of all that is great and noble in Spanish national life, fighting for Christian civilisation; and on the other the forces of anti-Christ and destructive Communism, which aim at destroying every vestige of religion in Spain and wiping out the name of God Himself.

Is Ireland's wholehearted sympathy for Franco's cause to be wondered at? Can the gesture of the Irish brigade, made despite every obstacle that arose, be wondered at?

The Irish Dominican Father, Rev. Paul O'Sullivan, Rector, Irish Church, Lisbon, who addressed a section passing through, expressed the highest feelings and aspirations of every volunteer in the brigade.

"You are going to fight, not for human glory, not in a human cause, however sacred and dear it may be," he said, "you are fighting in God's holy name, for God's glory, in God's defence, to save our holy Faith, to save Christianity, to save the world from the fiendish atrocities which have been perpetrated in Russia, in Mexico and now in Spain.

"You have elected, dear friends, to fight in the holiest war that was ever waged on this earth.

"Of this there can be no doubt, for never in the history of this sad world did human monsters rise up in battle against God Himself, never did men dare to make war against the Almighty personally, directly, with such satanical hate.

"The Bolshevists against whom you go to fight have in their insane fury declared that they will hurl the Creator from His throne. What demoniacal blasphemy!

"Give a noble Christian example which will fill our boys at home with enthusiasm and bring them in thousands to fight by your side in this holiest of causes.

"Why will not thousands of men from every nation flock to this holy, sacred fight for God, religion and civilisation? Is it not better to fight these monsters abroad, and with a people and for a country dear to us for many reasons, than to wait for them to come and perpetrate the same appalling crimes and atrocities in our land that they have perpetrated elsewhere?

"Why wait to see our churches burned, our priests and nuns butchered, our women—your mothers and wives and sisters—violated and mutilated by these fiends in human form, who openly threaten to bring equal ruin on us all?"

"Go, then, dear friends, and God be with you."

Chapter V

THE COMMUNIST PLAN FOR SPAIN — HOW THE PLAN WAS PURSUED — WAR AGAINST GOD — THE ILLEGITIMATE CORTES — RED RULE

THE TRAGEDY of Spain was inspired by Lenin, though written in the blood and tears of the Spanish people.

During 1931-32 Russia drew up a plan or "Manual of Action" for Spain, which gradually came into operation with the burning of churches and convents, the murder of priests and nuns. Propaganda, against religion in general, and the Catholic Church in particular, was flooded amongst the peasant workers. I have been told by an Irish girl who was at school in Madrid at the time that university professors lectured on the doctrines of Karl Marx and Lenin and supplied their students, free of charge, with text-books explaining that religion was the "opium of the people", a poisoned potion prepared by a capitalist Church, such that when men had partaken of it they would be satisfied to live in misery and poverty, dreaming and hoping of a better world to come. God was a mere figment of the imagination. There was no God, neither had man a divine destiny. Science and modern scholarship, it was said, had long since disproved the existence of a Supreme Being. The idea of God must be uprooted and everything savouring of Christianity destroyed if the Spanish Soviet State was to be established on the Russian model.

The Minister for Justice in the Red Government of Spain, Garcia Olives, speaking at a meeting on December 31st, 1936, at which the Minister for Propaganda presided, summed up the doctrine thus: "Man comes from the beasts, and that is why his reactions are those of a beast. Why punish prostitution? It should be legally organised."

So, instead of the ancient faith of their fathers, the youth of Spain began slowly to imbibe the doctrines on the rights of man, free love, and the negation of private property, which were the foundation stones of that terrestrial paradise where all men were rich, free and equal.

"Our school system," said the Minister for Education, "must aim at releasing the growing generation from obedience to parents or to conscience." Writing to a congress in Moscow he said: "Your struggle against religion is also ours. It is our duty to make Spain a land of militant atheists. All Spanish churches are being transformed into Communist schools and colleges."

At the seventh Communist "International" the Spanish delegate, Ventura, had said: "Under the banner of Lenin and Stalin we in Spain shall march forward to victory with our heads held high." This congress resolved that "The revolution cannot be effective so long as family life and family ties remain."

Spain gave to herself a new Constitution, drawn up by a committee of which the chair was filled by Señor Jiminez de Asua, who had just returned from Moscow. The republican Government was then in office. Strikes and street fighting became general. At a meeting of the Executive of the Communist International held in Moscow the Spanish delegate was able to say, to the great joy of M. Stalin, who presided: "The prerequisites of a revolutionary crisis are being created at a rapid pace in Spain." That pace was not fast enough however, for Moscow declared: "These strikes and economic deadlocks must be converted into genuine revolutionary struggles to such a degree that the Spanish proletariat has never witnessed before.

The Communist party must take over and control the entire cultural and spiritual life."

In 1932, the second year of the republican Government, Soviet propaganda was further translated into action all over the country. At Sollana, in the province of Alicante, a Soviet Republic was proclaimed. The town hall was set on fire in which perished the municipal archives; the church, with all its precious property, was razed to the ground. The mob cheered each outrage, and by the time the Government troops arrived the town was practically in a shambles.

In Málaga a number of bomb outrages took place, with great loss of life. In Seville, where there was a Communist strike, thousands entrenched themselves in the principal buildings armed with bombs, rifles and machine-guns. The peasants were holding mass meetings addressed by Communist experts. The red flag with the hammer and sickle was everywhere raised, and the *Internationale* resounded throughout the land. Outrage followed outrage without any of the perpetrators being brought to justice. Russia still poured in her poisonous propaganda, and hatred for everything Christian became more and more apparent. The wayside shrines and crosses, a characteristic feature of the Spanish countryside, some of them dating from the twelfth century, were smashed. A group of young men attacked a procession of the Blessed Sacrament at Cogollo de Veja. The priest who carried the monstrance was seriously wounded, and had just time to consume the Sacred Host before the monstrance was smashed against the pavement.

With delight Moscow announced: "Revolution is taking place in Spain, and the mass movement is showing tendencies to develop into an armed revolt of the people."

The importance attached to the creation of a Soviet Spain appeared from an announcement by M. Shvernik, Secretary of the Soviet Trade Union Council, that a grant of £479,000 was made to the Spanish Front.

Then came the rising in the Asturias. In Oviedo the interior of the beautiful cathedral was hacked to pieces, and the world-famous library of forty thousand volumes, with its priceless manuscripts, was destroyed. Priests were burned alive in the public parks after being subjected to the most bestial treatment.

The miners' rising was planned and engineered by Moscow. The "first Soviet Republic in Spain" came into existence after the historic buildings, with their treasures in works of art and books, were completely destroyed. Throughout Spain, then, a general strike was proclaimed in sympathy with the Asturian mob. The year came to a close amid chaos from Cadiz to Madrid, and from Madrid to the Bay of Biscay.

And what has Moscow to say about it all? "The events that took place represent not the end of the struggle for power for the Soviet, but only its beginning—the idea which the Spanish proletariat had been lacking for years has penetrated at last into the minds of the masses, and is supported by large sections of the intellectuals."

In February, 1936, the elections were held. The Popular Front were defeated, yet when the Cortes assembled it was found they outnumbered the Right Wing parties.

Señor Zamora, who was the first President of the Republic in 1931, and President at the time of the elections, showed himself a partisan of the extreme Left Wing during his whole period of office. Writing on the election, however, he says: "At the urge of irresponsible agitators, the mob seized the ballot papers, with the result that many false returns were sent in." In València and Cuenca the ballot boxes were deliberately broken open by parties of Reds, and the election of their candidates was declared. Further, the Popular Front appointed the committee entrusted with the task of counting the votes, who made sure that the Popular Front had a good majority in the Cortes, for when they came to count the votes, they found that it was not such a popular front after all.

In a certain constituency, the Popular Front, with 30,000 votes less than the Opposition, won ten seats out of thirteen. Altogether the Popular Front polled 214,000 fewer votes than the parties of the Right, and 554,000 fewer than the Right and

Centre parties together. Yet the official result of the election was: Popular Front—256; Right and Centre—217.

Not content with this, the Government set up a committee to "verify the elections". "In certain provinces," writes the ex-President of the Republic, "where the Opposition had been victorious, the elected candidates were deprived of their seats, and defeated candidates proclaimed Deputies."

The final official result was issued as: Popular Front—295; Right and Centre—177.

In their joint letter, the Cardinals, Archbishops and Bishops of Spain declare: "The votes of whole provinces had been cancelled at will, thus corrupting in its origin the legitimacy of parliament."

I think this should dispose of the contention that the Red Government was the popularly elected Government of the people of Spain. This Government, against which General Franco revolted, had not legitimate, but only usurped authority. The creation of fraud and violence, it did not represent the Spanish people. It was never capable of governing, and had no right to govern.

Immediately after the elections the President of the Republic was dismissed, judges, high officials of the army, police and public services who did not openly proclaim themselves as Red adherents were removed from office. In the barracks leaflets were distributed inciting the soldiers to murder their officers, and the latter were assaulted in the streets and public places. Important positions such as those of civil governors, mayors of cities, chief magistrates, were filled, not by men previously indicted for political offences but often by common criminals.

Even before the results of the election were known, the Asturian miners who had taken part in the rising of the previous October were released together with the most notorious criminals in the Spanish jails. These were armed by the Government with modern weapons. Russian experts arrived to train and lead these tried desperadoes, who were given a free hand to murder and loot. They were called "police" officially, so as to give the

Communists the necessary machinery with which to wreak their will.

Week by week the power of the "proletariat" showed itself. Acts of violence went unpunished and the growing impotency of the Popular Front to govern manifested itself from the beginning. Chaos and disorder spread like a disease throughout the country until life and property were at the mercy of the mob.

The clouds of revolution which had so long hung over the unhappy land now burst with indescribable fury, and all the floodgates of human passion were opened. The hour had struck when everything Christian was to be destroyed in the flames of Red revolution, and above the smouldering ruins was to be created the new paradise of the proletariat.

The Marquis Merry del Val, brother of the late Cardinal Merry del Val, and former Spanish Ambassador in London, who had been living in Spain all the time, and made a special study of conditions, writes:

> "The reign of terror began with the accession to power of the so-called Popular Front on 17th February, 1936. From February to July 18th, when General Franco rose in revolt, 251 churches were burned or blown up, 269 persons were murdered, 1,278 wounded. This brought the number of churches destroyed *before* the outbreak of war up to one thousand. It is calculated that since then from fourteen thousand to twenty thousand priests, monks and *religieuse* have been murdered, thousands of them after the most cruel physical and moral torture.

> "Not a parish priest is alive now in the four Catalan provinces, eleven bishops were murdered—some of them burned alive. All the churches in that portion of Spain occupied by the Reds have been burned, with the exception of Barcelona Cathedral, and Mass is no longer said. In Madrid alone the local authorities give the number of persons murdered as thirty-six thousand and in Barcelona the number of assassinations vies with that of Madrid, if it does not surpass it.

Four hundred priests were murdered in Barcelona alone. The dead body of the Bishop of Jaca was disinterred by women, who divested it of its shroud, hung it from a tree, poured petrol over it and after setting it on fire, danced around it in a ring. People were publicly flogged naked for refusing to blaspheme, and afterwards beheaded with axes. The police, by order, did not lift a finger to prevent these criminal acts, but if some courageous citizen attempted to defend his fellow-creatures he was instantly arrested. The fire brigade had similar instructions. To shout 'Long live Spain' was to court death. 'Viva Russia' was the popular slogan."

"Not for the past twelve months has anyone been either married or buried with Christian rites in this city of over a million people—nearly all brought up as Christians," the *Times* correspondent in Madrid reported. Boys and girls dressed as priests and nuns may be seen on the streets carrying buckets of dirty water in mockery of holy water.

The originator of crimes of these types was the notorious Béla Kun. He had tried his hand in Italy, Germany, Austria and Hungary, but failed. It is said that he is now awaiting trial for high treason against the Soviet Government of Russia.

Were there no God-fearing people to raise their voices against all this, it may be asked. The answer is that the masses had been robbed by assassination of their natural leaders, and left a prey to Soviet propaganda and terrorism.

Tragic accounts of the bloodshed were given to the Cortes by that great Catholic, Sotelo, leader of the Right Wing party, in the hope of influencing the Government to take action. He was shouted down, threatened with death. His speedy end was publicly foretold by the self-styled *La Pasionaria* ("Passion Flower"), a notorious woman, who was responsible for many of the crimes against the priests and nuns. Prominent members of the Right Wing were blacklisted by the Communists' murder gang, and the noble and fearless Sotelo was taken from his home in the darkness of night by fifteen members of the newly-created police force, in a police tender, No. 17. His dead body was found in a cemetery next morning, shockingly mutilated. On the same morning the homes of other Right Wing leaders, including Gil Robles, were visited, but, fortunately, the leaders managed to escape the assassins.

The murder gangs were now urged "to follow up recent successes, by applying methods studied at first hand in the Soviet Union". The organ of the Communist International declared: "The iron is hot in Spain, and must be struck now, sharply and boldly."

Soon the Government, which had never made the slightest attempt to govern, was being replaced by local Soviets, tribunal parodies and Marxist militia; composed, for the great part, of criminals of all sorts and degrees.

Black lists of persons to be "eliminated" were prepared by local Communists—the bishop's name usually headed the list, followed next by the priests. One Communist leader, while in the act of killing a priest, was approached by the people to save their pastor. His reply was: "We have orders to root up all their seed."

The Spanish delegates to the last Moscow Congress reported: "We have surpassed Russia, as the Church in Spain is now completely annihilated."

That the boasted annihilation would have been utterly complete but for Franco's rising is made clear in the joint letter of the Bishops of Spain. With this record of stark horror should be considered also, of course, the facts previously given of the atrocities committed before the outbreak of war. Of the Reds' campaign during the war the Bishops state:

"We calculate that about twenty thousand churches have been destroyed. The priests were hunted with dogs, they were pursued across the mountains, they were searched for with eagerness in every hiding place. The forms of murder took the character of horrible barbarity. Many have had their limbs amputated or have been dreadfully mutilated before being murdered; their eyes have been put out, their tongues cut out, they have been ripped open from top to bottom, burned or buried alive or chopped to death with axes.

"The greatest cruelty has been used against the ministers of God. For respect and charity we do not wish to give any more detailed account. The honour of women has not been respected, not even of those consecrated to God. Hundreds of prisoners tied together, as at Bilbao, have been given over to the mob, who murdered them in a most inhuman way.

"The hatred against Jesus Christ and the Blessed Virgin," continue the Bishops, "has reached paroxysm. In the slashed crucifixes, in the images of the Blessed Virgin bestially profaned, in the lampoons of Bilbao, in which the Mother of God is sacrilegiously blasphemed, in the vile literature of the Red trenches, in the repeated profanation of the Sacred Host, we can glimpse the hatred of hell incarnated.

"The profanation of sacred relics has been frightful. The bodies of St. Narcissus, St. Pascal Baylon, the Blessed Beatrice, St. Bernard, and others, have been destroyed or burnt. We do not blame the Spanish people," conclude the Bishops, "for anything more than having served as an instrument for the perpetration of these crimes. This hatred towards religion came from Russia. Let us say that when dying under the sanction of the law our Communists have been reconciled to God in their vast majority. This is a proof of the deceit of which our people have been the victims."

From this review the reader has seen the growth and spread of Communism in Spain, tended by the hand of Russia, and nurtured in the blood of the Spanish priests and people.

It was only in July, 1936, when all seemed lost, and the red flag seemed to have triumphed over the Cross, that God raised up, in the person of General Franco, a patriotic and God-fearing man to deliver Spain out of the hands of Satan and his Communist legionaries.

Chapter VI

ORGANISING THE BRIGADE — TRANSPORT PLAN — THE SET-BACK — MEETING WITH FRANCO

BACK in Dublin, after General Franco had accepted the offer of our Irish Brigade, I faced at once the rather formidable task of organisation.

Six thousand letters had to be acknowledged, and a form of application sent to each volunteer. On the return of these forms records were prepared by counties, showing the name, address, references, age, nationality and particulars of the applicants, military, professional and educational qualifications, whether married or single, having dependents. It was agreed with the Spanish higher command that the Brigade should be self-contained and officered by Irishmen, and as sufficient volunteers had offered their services to form a full brigade it was necessary to prepare a scheme of organisation accordingly. This involved selection of the most suitable officers and N.C.O.'s for brigade, battalion, company, platoon and section staffs, the personnel of rifle and machine-gun companies, the segregation and classification of the volunteers according to their experience and suitability for special corps, engineers, signals, supply, transport, first aid, military police. It was necessary to ensure, so far as possible, that men were physically fit for service, and arrangements were made for their medical examination at Dublin, Cork, and other centres before acceptance.

When the final selection had been made, each approved volunteer was notified, and advised to hold himself in readiness to travel on short notice. He was warned, too, that as the Brigade was entirely voluntary, no responsibility could be accepted for dependents, and that ranks previously held in the Irish Republican, the National, or British armies were not being recognised, all volunteers being regarded as of equal rank on leaving Ireland.

As only one bandera succeeded in reaching Spain only a small number of officers was required. A full brigade was anticipated, however, and it was necessary to make provision for a full complement of officers and N.C.O.'s. Accordingly, many volunteers with the experience and record entitling them to commissioned or non-commissioned rank had, perforce, to serve in the rank and file, but there was no grumble.

The organisation of the Brigade was, perhaps, the most difficult job I have ever undertaken, but with the help of willing workers at headquarters all obstacles were gradually surmounted.

Transport at once presented difficulties. There were no passenger ships for Spain or Portugal calling at Irish ports, and few at English ports, in the winter season. The fitting up of cargo ships for a week's sea journey for so many men would cost an enormous amount, and there was always the danger of an unreliable crew. Various firms, mostly British, quoted for the job, but the price was in all cases prohibitive. I received some fantastic offers.

It was Señor la Cierva, statesman and aeronautical inventor, who eventually arranged our transport, travelling to Spain of his own accord to do so.

It was not generally known that Señor la Cierva was one of General Franco's right-hand men. He held no rank in the army nor in the Cabinet, yet he was a power behind the nationalist throne—looking after Franco's interest in London, and various European capitals. From the first day we met he manifested the keenest interest in the proposed Irish Brigade. Having a remarkable knowledge of the historic links between Ireland and Spain, he was convinced from the outset that a distinct Irish unit, however small, fighting on the side of the Nationalists would be an asset of immense value.

On his return to London from Spain he sent for me, and beaming with delight, announced he had chartered one of Spain's best ships, the *Domino*, and had it fitted out with cabins and sleeping accommodation for one thousand men. Nicholas Franco, Secretary of State, and brother of the Generalissimo, had travelled with him to the port of Vigo to supervise the preparation of the ship, supplies of food, and so on. "Real Irish menus, and no olive oil," he said, by way of joke, knowing my antipathy to the latter. The ship was fitted with anti-aircraft guns, and a Spanish Admiral was to travel in charge, with an English-speaking staff of stewards. Speed tests had been carried out so that the exact time of the arrival of the ship at an Irish port could be intimated to me. La Cierva knew it was my desire that as our cars were moving into the port the ship should be moving into harbour.

Afterwards I learned that a surprise had been arranged—that Nicholas Franco would himself travel on board as a gesture of appreciation—so highly did he esteem Irish aid.

It was also arranged that a fleet of planes should meet the *Domino* out at sea, and that on arrival at Vigo, the Cardinal Primate should be present to give his blessing to the Irish Brigade. From Vigo we were to travel by special train to Burgos, where the convent schools and grounds were placed at our disposal by the nuns.

The *Domino* was due to reach Passage East—five miles from Waterford City—at 2 a.m., on Friday, 16th October, 1936.

It was now 5th October. I flew back to Dublin that afternoon, and the next few days were occupied in the preparation of the final list of accepted volunteers. Owing to our Government's adherence to the Non-Intervention Pact, with which I shall deal in its international aspect later, it was necessary to keep our plans secret.

We could not, therefore, disclose the place, date or hour of embarkation to the selected volunteers until the last moment, nor could we hire buses or cars in advance. Also because of the non-political character of the brigade, the activities of the National Corporate Party, which I had been directing for some time, were suspended and we had no organisation available to assist us.

In three days, however, we had a reliable keyman appointed for each county, and two for the larger counties. These keymen accepted arduous and responsible duties at a moment's notice, many travelled to Dublin for instructions and special couriers drawn from the volunteers in Dublin brought instructions to the others. The keymen, without exception, carried out their work at this and later stages with credit to themselves and to my entire satisfaction.

In my interview with General Mola, I had learned of the difficulties in procuring uniforms for the troops owing to the factories and textiles being in the hands of the Reds. From the disciplinary point of view, it was desirable that there should be some uniformity in dress for our volunteers, and I found it necessary to place hurried orders in Dublin for a thousand standard green shirts and a thousand standard caps. They were got ready in time and were worn *en route*, during training, and some volunteers still retain them as souvenirs. Many of the men who had volunteered were poor, and unable to provide themselves with the bare travelling necessities; these had to be procured. It was necessary, too, to arrange for a brigade headquarters in Dublin, with a staff, as a rallying centre.

For all this, money was necessary, and notwithstanding my other responsibilities I was obliged to turn my attention to this problem. I issued an urgent appeal for funds for the Irish Crusade against Communism. Many people adopted that attitude of apathy which afflicted Spain in the early days of Communist activity in that country. However, we got a little money from those who could least afford it, and who had least to say. Another immediate obstacle was overcome.

An experienced sea captain from Passage East accepted responsibility for signalling and piloting the *Domino* into harbour, and for arranging a fleet of motor boats to convey the volunteers to the ship.

On October 10th, I travelled to London again, to satisfy myself as to final arrangements and was assured that everything was working out according to plan. I came back to Dublin and issued my final instructions to all keymen, of which the following, sent to Co. Sligo, is typical:

SECRET.

Mr. GALLAGHER,

Arrangements are complete for departure of Irish Brigade for Spain. We leave by ship from Passage East, five miles east of Waterford City, at 2 a.m. Friday next, 16th October, 1936.

You will immediately make arrangements to collect men according to the list already sent you, and you will travel from Sligo via Athlone, Roscrea, Thurles, Clonmel, Carrick-on-Suir and thence on south side of river Suir to destination—leaving Waterford City on left. Men carrying ash plants in their right hands will be on your line of route near Clonmel, Carrick-on-Suir and Waterford, to give you further guidance if you require their help.

You will leave from Sligo Thursday afternoon or evening in sufficient time to arrive at one o'clock on the morning of Friday at Passage East, and if possible you will time your speed to ensure that you do not arrive before that hour.

You will see that as far as possible the cars make no stop at any town during journey, and that under no circumstances are there stops for refreshments at any place. If refreshments are required they should be carried. When passing through towns absolute silence is to be maintained.

You will put a responsible man in charge of each car who will act under your instructions, and who will be given name of port and time for arrival when car is ready to move off. Under no circumstances is the port to be revealed to anyone until you are ready to leave.

It is absolutely essential that the men in first car of your contingent can be relied on implicitly. I would suggest you travel in the last car so that you can ensure all is well ahead and that nobody is being left behind. If any of your men have a knowledge of driving distribute them in the various cars in case they are required.

You will consider these instructions as final and act on them. I rely on you to get your men to the port, and at appointed time, no matter what efforts may be made to prevent you.

14/10/36.

It was now 7 p.m. on the evening of 14th October. Everything was complete, the final instructions had been issued and I was at home packing my bags and arranging to close up my house, when the doorbell rang.

It was a courier from Spain with a message from General Franco to the effect that owing to the reports received from the Non-Intervention Committee then sitting in London it was decided to postpone the sailing of the *Domino* for Ireland.

I had got some hard knocks in my time; this was the most severe of all. What was to be done? I sent the courier back to London by the 9 p.m. mail steamer from Dun Laoghaire to ask La Cierva to await me in London next forenoon.

How was I to cancel the arrangements already completed? Few if any of my keymen were on the 'phone, and I could not expect the police to deliver messages for me all over the country. I had given my staff an evening off, after an arduous month of working at high pressure day and night. I managed to find my secretary, Captain Walsh, who was resting at his home, and brought him back to the office, where we got out a cancellation notice.

Many of the volunteers had already left their homes for the county centres, and some were visiting friends to make their *adieux*. Money was scarce and we could not send out cars. In the few hours we had left we succeeded however in notifying all the counties except Mayo. Jack Moran and his party were on their way to Passage East and reached there at 1 a.m. according to plan, only to find the little village asleep.

I left for London next morning, but La Cierva had already gone to Spain, and I was advised to stay for a few days to await his return or a message from him. Having received no news, I set out for Salamanca—Franco's headquarters—via Paris and the frontier near Irun. With the Military Governor of Irun I inspected the sorry wreckage of that once prosperous town, now a blackened monument to Red hate.

After a visit to San Sebastián, I went to Fuenterrabia, where I was the guest of Mr. Walter Meade, one of the best-known sportsmen in Spain, whose father was from Co. Wicklow. Early next day I travelled to Salamanca. On the route which skirted the Bilbao front in places, were many battle-scarred towns and villages, and I was held up for some time at one point where soldiers were retrieving six big guns abandoned in ditches by the Reds in their flight to the west a few days before. At Burgos I halted to pay a call on the Civil Government, and some acquaintances whom I had met during the last visit.

On reaching Salamanca I went direct to General Franco's headquarters in the Bishop's Palace, and the Generalissimo received me at once. It was our first meeting. There too was Señor la Cierva and the discussion as I entered the office was about our Irish Brigade.

General Franco expressed his very sincere regret that it became necessary to upset all our arrangements. He spoke most feelingly of Ireland, and expressed his high appreciation of our efforts to aid Spain.

I told him of the intense disappointment his message to me had caused to the Irish volunteers.

With some emotion he said: "Spain is first, and after Spain Ireland is next in my esteem."

Reports had reached him, he explained, that Russia had threatened to break with the Non-Intervention Committee, which in effect meant that she would continue the supply of men and arms to the Reds. This did not cause him any surprise, but he could not give Russia any pretext, and the arrival of an Irish Brigade in Spain would certainly supply her with an excuse to carry out her threat—it would be playing into her hands.

I appreciated the difficulties of the international situation confronting Franco, and keenly as I felt the disappointment I agreed with him that he had no option but to act as he did.

Were it possible to avoid it, General Franco would not have accepted the services of one single foreign soldier. I discussed the whole matter with him. "I accepted responsibility," he said, "to liberate my country from Spanish Marxism. Now it would appear that the Marxists of Europe are concentrating on Spain. My task is formidable, but even yet—if there are no further arrivals—I have sufficient faith in the army to believe that we can deal with the situation without outside aid."

I may add that there were no foreign troops in Franco's victorious march from Seville to Salamanca, or at the relief of the Alcázar. At that time there were upwards of a hundred thousand Spaniards under arms on his side. Those who fought against him at Irun and San Sebastián were almost entirely foreign—French and Russian—while Franco can boast that he took these towns with his own Requetes from Nevada.

Having explained the situation, as I have indicated, General Franco advised me to stay in Spain for a few days to await developments. He issued instructions that I was to be received as a guest of the nation, and a special suite at the Grand Hotel was placed at my disposal. I was issued with a military car for my own use, and given a permit to visit the various fronts.

Next morning I visited Salamanca's cathedral, the ancient Irish College and the University. In the afternoon, accompanied by the Duke of Algeciras, who had been assigned to me as liaison officer, the Count San Esteban de Camongo, Captain Medrano—of General Franco's personal staff—Captain Meade, Captain Gunning and an escort, I left to visit the Madrid front. Our party travelled first to Ávila, and then by narrow mountain roads to Cebreros, where fierce lighting had cleared the hills of Reds only a week or so before. A pause here and there to examine their elaborate trench systems, machine-gun posts, and dugouts confirmed the impression that the Reds, through lack of morale, had failed to hold what were almost impregnable positions. Through Maqueda, where the boastful *No pasaran*—they shall not pass—of the Reds was still legible on the walls, through loop-holed villages, whose defenders having murdered the priests and desecrated the churches, had fled before the advancing Nationalists, I came at nightfall to Toledo, shadowed by the grim ruins of the Alcázar. Here I was received by Carlist and military guards of honour, and welcomed by the Military Governor, in whose headquarters apartments had been prepared for my party.

Next morning, accompanied by the Colonel in charge of the Toledo garrison, I drove to the Palace to pay my respects to Archbishop Goma y Tomas, Cardinal Primate of Spain. His Eminence received me with the greatest affection. In the course of an interview lasting for an hour and a half, he expressed again and again the joyful gratitude of Catholic Spain to Catholic Ireland for its sympathy and support. His Eminence said that at least one bright spot in the dark clouds hanging over his country that day was that the opportunity was so gladly availed of by Ireland to renew the historic ties between the two nations in defence of Christianity.

Cardinal Goma then showed me over his home, pointing out the desecration done while it had been used as a Red headquarters, and showed me "receipts" left for the priceless cathedral treasures that had been plundered. In Toledo alone one hundred and twenty priests had been murdered during the red terror; only those who had been absent on vacation, as the Primate himself was, having escaped.

After a visit to the beautiful cathedral, which had escaped destruction only because the Red chiefs locked it against the mob, while they themselves were pillaging the treasury, we went to the Alcázar. There I heard the stirring account of the siege already given. Leaving the Alcázar I inspected the shaft which Red miners had made to dynamite the fortress, and then, with a special escort of Civil Guards, who had been in the Alcázar garrison, departed for the Madrid front.

Burned out armoured cars, lorries and wrecked Red barricades marked the road to Yungos, where General Varela had his field headquarters. After a call on the General, who received us hospitably, we went to the village of Umanes, a mile from the front line. From the church tower, and without glasses, we got our first view of Madrid. It looked pretty and peaceful lying white in the afternoon sunshine. Those of our party who knew the city well pointed out to me the capital's chief landmarks.

The church in which we were, like others in the villages through which we had passed, was a sorry sight. It had been wrecked inside, and the altar in particular had been vilely desecrated. The least offensive act of sacrilege had been to use the church as a slaughter house. The skins and offal of sheep used to feed the Red militia were still lying around the sanctuary floor, for they had evacuated the village only that morning.

From Umanes we went to Parla, where the Nationalist artillery was in position. The village was being shelled by two batteries of artillery, and bombarded by Red planes. About five hundred yards in front the Nationalist front line, supported by armoured cars, was moving on under heavy fire in the long drive that had begun that morning on the other side of Umanes.

At Toledo, on the return journey, I was approached by three young officers of the Alcázar garrison who offered their services as my personal escort on my return to Spain. Knowing, as I did so well, the story of their gallantry, I regarded their offer as a great honour.

Back again at Salamanca I had a long conference with General Franco and his staff. Señor la Cierva was also present.

Reports had reached their headquarters while I was visiting the battlefields that Russians and Frenchmen were still pouring into the Red army by land, sea and air. The futility and hypocrisy of the Non-Intervention Pact had been more than adequately confirmed and I was authorised to proceed with the brigade scheme. Circumstances forced General Franco to realise that he was the central figure in a struggle not only for Spain, but for world Christianity.

Chapter VII

ARMED INTERVENTION IN SPAIN — WHY THE PACT? — THE PACT DISHONOURED — ATTITUDE OF THE NATIONS

B UT FOR RUSSIA there would be no civil war in Spain. But for the armed intervention of Russia and France neither Italy nor Germany would have intervened. Russia's activities in Spain began long ago. Sixteen years ago Lenin declared that Spain would become the second Soviet State in Europe and since then his successors have worked persistently to give effect to his prophecy.

Already I have told of the vast amounts sent from Moscow to be expended in Spain on Communist propaganda. From 1931 to 1936 Russian ships also brought munitions in surreptitiously, either direct from Russian ports, or through Mexico, Russia's western ally. Since February, 1936, ships laden with guns, tanks, fighting planes and other modern war equipment arrived openly. According to the Paris *Matin*, "These more recent cargoes were of shells, bombs, whippet tanks, aerial torpedoes, plant for the manufacture of gas, and everything necessary for chemical warfare. Teams of chemists, engineers and aviators travelled on the ships. Thus," adds the *Matin*, "Moscow has a powerful arsenal for world revolution at the disposal of Antonov Avesenko, Russian chief of the international Red army in Spain."

The greater part of the military stores mentioned arrived in Barcelona during the week ending Sunday, 15th November, 1936—many months after Russia had signed the Non-Intervention Pact with France, Britain, the Irish Free State and other countries. On March 1st, 1937, a consignment from Russia included one hundred heavy tanks, five hundred medium tanks, two thousand light tanks, four thousand machine-guns and three hundred planes with pilots. No fewer than fifty thousand rifles with appropriate ammunition left Mexico City for Spain on the liner *Magallanes* alone. Another Mexican shipment officially reported was of arms weighing fifteen hundred tons for the Red Government.

Much of the Russian supplies have been paid for, because Communist thievery on a gigantic scale has been carried out from the beginning. Priceless works of art, paintings, and other treasures taken from the pillaged monasteries and museums have been shipped to Soviet ports by the homeward-bound arms ships.

Madrid itself is held by an international army corps drawn from virtually every country in Europe, but chiefly from Russia, and commanded by Russian officers. The prisoners taken by General Varela on this front are mostly Russians, with some Czechoslovaks, German Jews and Frenchmen, but no Spaniards.

General Mola, too, had shown me arms captured from the Reds, which included those in official use in almost every country in Europe today.

Under the generals Kleber and Miaja are hundreds of Russian colonels and other officers, thousands of Russian N.C.O.'s and men. General Kleber by the way, is a Russian Jew, whose real name is Lazar Feket.

For some reason, probably to impress their comrades there, the Russians as a rule have travelled through France and thence across the frontier into Spain. They are usually accompanied by women camp followers, who are held responsible for many of the revolting crimes against priests, nuns and Spanish girls. Illuminating was the experience of Miss Anderson, war correspondent for the *New York American*, who wrote on June 13th, 1937:

"When arrested I demanded to be taken before the Spanish Government. The twenty-three-year-old female Red commandant replied 'Government! This pistol is Government. Who do you think you are talking to anyhow? Do you know who I am? Do you know how many people I have already killed? I have killed one hundred and eighty-nine.'"

Béla Kun paid particular attention to the province of Catalonia, where his scheme was to place a Russian leader in charge of the local Anarchists and Communists in each "division"—an area corresponding to a parish here. He had local supporters trained in the use of arms, but his principal mission was to spread the doctrine of Communism amongst the youth in the towns, who in turn acted as agents to instruct the semi-illiterate peasants. He was plentifully supplied with money, so that Catalonia became for all practical purposes a Soviet Republic with Barcelona as the seat of Government.

When we consider what has taken place behind the shield of the Non-Intervention Pact Committee, is it not straining our credulity to expect us to believe that the Government of Russia would act honourably in any international arrangement?

In France, too, the Pact had been more honoured in the breach than in the observance, though the French Government was its initiator. The French Communists, with the approval or complacent connivance of the Government, transported men and war material, including bombing planes, across the Spanish frontier, to aid their comrades even to a greater extent than did Russia.

The Pact did not in any way lessen these activities. Even while France was calling the nations of Europe to conclave for discussion and enforcement of the Pact, M. Blum's own newspaper was urging the formation of a national council to mobilise volunteers for Spain, and recruiting was going on openly in every city and town in France. Daily, trains and lorries of French Communists equipped with modern weapons of warfare were openly crossing into Spain. The factories and workshops continued turning out war material at high pressure for the Red Government. After the signing of the Pact according to *Candide*, a French weekly, the three biggest factories in France—the Bloch, the Brandt and the Lioré Olivier—were permitted to work day and night shifts to turn out war planes, guns and shells to "help our Spanish comrades".

The Spanish Ambassador in Paris still acted as recruiter for the Fronte Popular. From August to November, 1936, two steady streams of volunteers passed into Spain—one by the Catalonian frontier on land, and the other via Marseilles-Barcelona on sea. By the end of that November it was estimated that there were twenty thousand French volunteers on the Catalonia and València fronts alone.

On July 20th, 1936, the Spanish Ambassador in Paris had visited M. Blum, then Prime Minister, with a request to send at once to Barcelona thirteen bombing planes, fifty machine-guns with two million machine-gun cartridges, one million Lebel cartridges, eight ·75 field guns with appropriate shells, and twenty thousand gas bombs. A Cabinet Meeting was called and the French Government agreed to meet this demand. The counsellor of the Spanish Embassy and the military attaché resigned rather than be a party to this transaction, and wrote to the Press explaining why. A few days later both were ordered to leave French territory.

On August 6th, 1936, a few days before the signing of the Non-Intervention Pact, according to *Action Française*, the French War Minister, M. Daladier, issued an order for the immediate transport to Barcelona of eight ·75 field guns and one thousand six hundred shells, two thousand rifles, fifty machine-guns with six million cartridges, and ten thousand aeroplane bombs. These were loaded in the *Ciudad de Cadiz*. On August 9th the French Government admitted having exported arms to Spain and added that such exports would now cease.

On August 30th, September 2nd and 4th, October 8th, 9th and 14th, various consignments of arms were nevertheless sent by land and sea to the Spanish Reds. Up to the end of October France had sent one hundred and twenty-nine planes to Spain, of which eighty-three were war planes of the French Government fleet. The majority of these were sent in October, some months after the signing of the Pact. Appeals for funds to purchase war materials for the Spanish Red militia continued to appear in many Paris newspapers, and up to the end of October the amount of money subscribed amounted to eight million francs.

Letters addressed to places in Nationalist Spain, whether posted in France or passing through France, were held up by the French postal authorities and sent to Barcelona. The *Écho de Paris* of 12th November, 1936, says: "Very often these letters contain indications which make it easy for these assassins to carry out atrocious reprisals."

The now famous letter of July 25th, 1936, from Señor Hernando de los Rios, since appointed Ambassador to U.S.A., to Señor Giral, then Prime Minister in Red Spain, has been widely published already, and I shall only quote a few extracts from it. It was written only nine days before the French Government issued its proposals for the Non-Intervention Pact. "Last night when I arrived in Paris from London, I was summoned urgently," he wrote, "to the home of the head of the Government (M. Blum). Four Ministers were present, whose views are of the greatest weight, owing to the departments over which they preside.

"I was told by one Minister that all the material—planes, machines and guns—was ready and could be sent away in the morning. I retired to sleep, and one hour later I was sent for urgently by the Air Minister, M. Cot. He informed me that it was impossible to convince the Minister for External Affairs that it would not be irregular to have French machines flown to Spain by French aviators.

"When I went this morning to the Air Ministry everything was going well, but when I arrived at the firm the difficulties seemed insurmountable. The Press campaign over the publication of the reasons for the resignations of the counsellor of the Spanish Embassy and the military attaché looms so big that when Blum went this morning to see the President of the French Republic he found him perturbed and he ordered an extraordinary Cabinet Meeting for 4 p.m.

"From 2:30 p.m. until 3:45 p.m. I have been with the Prime Minister. Never have I seen him so profoundly moved. 'I shall maintain my position at all costs and in spite of all risks', he said. 'We must help Spain. How? We shall see.'

"The resolution of the Cabinet was to avoid delivery from Government to Government, but to grant us the necessary permits so that private firms may deliver the machines to us. They anticipate that we shall be able to take the aeroplanes out of the country on Monday or Tuesday. The Potez planes will be built. I shall arrange for the safe passage of the bombs. For arms I think we can only deal with Hotchkiss."

Well may it be asked, what right had the French Government to ask others to observe the Non-Intervention agreement?

Sir Charles Petrie, in the *English Review*, concisely puts the position in saying that, "While officially adopting, a policy of non-intervention in Spain, France has done everything in its power to help the Reds. Were it not for such aid Franco would long since be master of Spain."

On the other hand, Mr. Brockway, the British Socialist leader, said, in March, 1937: "I cannot tell publicly all I know, but when the story of the Spanish war comes to be written, it will be found that the assistance the French revolutionary Left party has given to the Spanish workers in the way of supplies and enabling volunteers to go through, has been equal to that of any party in the world."

Britain, as usual, has been playing a shrewd part all through. At the very outset Italy and Germany proposed measures to confine the conflict to Spanish territory. The proposition was pooh-poohed by England and France. Why? Was it because those countries supporting the Communists had not given full effect to their plans? From the day when non-intervention was first mooted the Governments of Russia and France worked hard to rush men and war materials to Spain. Then, when it was thought, apparently, that the Reds were sufficiently strengthened by men and arms to crush Franco, the French Government backed by the British Government sponsored a non-intervention scheme and hurried the nations into a Pact the terms of which they themselves had rejected a few weeks before.

The Pact was dishonoured from the beginning. While the Non-Intervention Committee was sitting in London the Red newspapers in Spain were boasting of the arrival of hundreds of Russian tanks and Russian war planes. It is possible only to conclude that it was cunningly designed in the Communists' interest. It had become apparent that Italy and Germany might, for their own safety, take a hand in the business, so it was proposed to put a cordon round Spain, then await the annihilation of Franco's army, and the extension of the Communist campaign to Nationalist territory.

Italy and Germany were expected to look quietly on while Russia, aided by powerful allies, established a new Soviet State to embrace the whole of the Iberian Peninsula—for if General Franco were defeated Portugal too would be forced to surrender or become a shambles in a few weeks. With M. Blum and his Popular Front Government in office France could be relied upon to link up with the Soviet bloc.

Hitler, however, was well aware that Bolshevism brought Germany down to a fifth-rate power, and well nigh succeeded in making it bankrupt. Mussolini was well aware of the conditions existing in his own country when he was hailed as its deliverer from the designs of Russia. Were it not for Hitler and Mussolini, Germany and Italy would have had the blood bath which Spain is enduring today. They kept a close watch on developments in Spain and came to the conclusion that the time had arrived to put a stop to the Communist march through Europe, if their own nations were to survive. They offered to send men and armaments to General Franco. The offer was accepted. It is terrible to contemplate what the consequences might otherwise have been not only for Spain, but indeed for Europe.

In England there was strong support for the Spanish Communists, voiced chiefly through the trade unions. At the Trade Union Congress in September, 1937, Sir Walter Citrine said: "The English labour movement has never accepted the position of neutrality, and has never hesitated to reveal its complete solidarity with its Spanish comrades." A resolution was passed unanimously pledging support to the Reds. At a previous congress it was reported that a sum of £126,000 had been subscribed in aid of the Reds—the trade unions contributing over £37,000. This policy of course was in line with that of the International Federation of Trade Unions which at a conference held in March, 1937, passed the following resolution: "We have consistently and unconditionally given our wholehearted moral support to our Spanish comrades. We have given them material help in every possible form. We shall continue to make every effort to increase this support."

England's attitude is in many aspects difficult to understand, and the attitude of certain high dignitaries of the Church of England is not the least difficult. Sir Francis Lindley, G.C.M.G., C.B., in February, 1937, wrote: "The attitude of Home of our highly-placed divines is stupefying, and to me personally, as a lifelong member of the Church of England, revolting. I have cudgelled my brains in vain to find the explanation of their support of the so-called Government of Spain. I hesitate to accept the only logical explanation—that they do not regard the Catholic Church as a branch of Christianity, or professing Roman Catholics as entitled to the rights enjoyed by the rest of mankind."

There is nothing altruistic, to my mind, in England's attitude. Were it not for the rise of Italy and Germany she would be a full-blooded supporter of Franco.

If one travelled from San Sebastián to Oviedo a few years ago, one would see more Union Jacks than Spanish flags.

Because of trade relations, this part of Spain was closely linked up with Britain, and Britons had many interests there. Evidently she satisfied herself at the beginning of the war that Franco would or must be defeated. Indeed, even since, if we were to accept the B.B.C. news broadcasts, Franco has all the time been advancing backwards on the various fronts.

General Franco, however, with characteristic courage, called Britain's bluff in no uncertain manner. He demonstrated his strength by annexing Bilbao and Santander in quick succession. The Reds cannot be of much service to British interests in this section of Spain, and if her lucrative trade is to continue Britain is forced to recognise that it now belongs to Franco. Already discussions have taken place between Franco's Government and the British on trade matters, including the future of British-owned mines in Spain, and there has been an exchange of representatives between the two countries—a definite step by Britain towards the recognition of Franco's Government.

The number of English fighting for the Reds was comparatively few, the majority were made prisoners by General Franco, and, following representations made on their behalf, they were sent across the frontier. They gave glowing accounts of the kindness and consideration shown to them by the officers and soldiers of the Nationalist army, in contrast to that of the Red army. They did not enlist to fight, but as workmen in an engineer's corps and resented very much being put into infantry uniforms and rushed to the Madrid front without a day's training. There was quite a number of British planes on the Red side, and many of those brought down had English pilots.

Though Britain has no small share of responsibility for the establishment of the Soviet regime in Russia, and though she offered scant hospitality to the Queen of Spain—an English princess—when the royal family had to flee from the palace in Madrid before the fury of the Communists a few years ago, she has no great love for Communism. A divided and dependent Spain would, however, serve her interests. Franco is winning, and it is for Britain to wriggle out as best she can. Franco has said: "Naturally in the future, when Spain is once more free and independent, we will look with much more favour upon nations which have openly supported our patriotic movement rather than those which have openly opposed us, or chosen to adopt an indifferent attitude, waiting for the outcome of the war."

With her eye on the Mediterranean, Britain fears, too, that a strong, united Spain, allied perhaps with Italy and Germany, would make her position somewhat precarious there.

For Britain, as for Europe at large, non-intervention has been a miserable failure, where it has not been a cloak for Communist treachery.

The Non-Intervention Committee, like the League of Nations, has its wheels in a Communist ditch.

When the League met to discuss sanctions against Italy, the Russian, Litvinoff, occupied the chair. In September, 1937, when the war in Spain was under discussion in the League Assembly, Negrin, Premier of Communist Spain, was in the chair, and the representatives of great Powers, which have openly supported the Communists with men and munitions in their efforts to wipe out Christianity, were there to influence its decisions.

What progress in civilisation can such a League make?

Chapter VIII

THE BANDERA SETS OUT — CONDITIONS OF SERVICE — WHO WERE THE VOLUNTEERS — TROOPSHIP AT GALWAY

THE ALTERED PLANS for the Irish Brigade having been final-
ised with General Franco and his Salamanca headquarters,
I set out on my return journey to Ireland. I halted for a night at
the home in Biarritz of the former Spanish Minister to Ireland,
Señor Alvaraz d'Aguilar, and was received most hospitably. We
talked over conditions in Spain until far into the night. He left
next morning for San Sebastián to join the Nationalist forces,
after seeing me entrained for Paris, *en route* to Dublin.

I reached home on November 5th, and at once convened a
meeting of keymen from the various counties for Sunday,
November 8th, to explain to them the altered plans.

Thousands of men had made preliminary arrangements to
travel, and intense disappointment was expressed that provision
could not be made for larger contingents. It was reported that
hundreds of Irishmen resident in Britain had volunteered their
services and it was a matter of keen regret that it was not possible to include them.

At the conference I explained the main headings of agreement between General Franco and myself, which were, that:

The Irish volunteers would form banderas (battalions) of the Tercio or Spanish legion—the bandera to consist of eight hundred officers, N.C.O.'s and legionaires, each bandera would be self-contained so far as possible, and officered by Irishmen, the commander having an English-speaking Spanish A.D.C. or Adjutant. Attached to each of the four companies of the bandera there would be, if possible, a Spanish liaison officer, and a limited number of Spanish N.C.O.'s and privates capable of speaking English. Each Irish bandera would constitute a distinct unit, and in the event of further banderas arriving from Ireland all would operate together in the field and in the same column, provided the necessities of the campaign would not render it necessary to separate the banderas temporarily. No Irish bandera would be engaged against the Basque nationalists—this was at my request, but they could be employed on any other front. The pay would correspond to that of the same ranks in the Tercio. If Irish officers with the requisite technical qualifications were brought to Spain they would be entrusted with the command of columns embracing several banderas, all of which need not necessarily be Irish. The Irish units would follow their own system of military drill and ceremonial. Their food would approach as nearly as possible to that which they were accustomed to and would be cooked and served by their own staffs. They would have their own chaplains, doctors and nurses. I was to undertake the duties of Inspector-General of the Irish banderas, for which I would be directly responsible to the Generalissimo, and my rank would be that of Brigadier-General. I would have a Spanish adjutant in addition to an Irish adjutant. I requested a lower rank, and eventually accepted the rank assigned to me on condition that no salary or allowance whatever would be attached to it. The period of service would be for the duration of the war, or for six months—whichever was the shorter.

Having agreed on the main issues, General Franco left it to the staff and myself to work out details as to mode of travelling and so on. It had not been considered feasible that Irish volunteers should travel then on a special ship, and alternative arrangements had been made between Señor la Cierva and myself whereby small groups would travel weekly from Dublin to Liverpool by the ordinary steamers, from Liverpool to Lisbon by the ordinary weekly sailings, and thence by road transport into Spain. Each individual volunteer would travel unarmed and in mufti, purchase his own ticket and when he reached Spain make personal application for admission to the legion. To facilitate matters, one volunteer in each group would be selected to take responsibility for travel arrangements, and would carry a document for identification purposes with his own photo at the top, and underneath a list of the volunteers travelling with him.

The volunteers carrying out these arrangements could not be said to infringe Irish or international law, and it was this which no doubt prompted the Free State Government to put through its Non-Intervention measure soon afterwards.

Our Irish Brigade members would not be allowed to embark at Liverpool for Lisbon without passports, and accordingly the keymen were instructed to advise volunteers to procure passports without delay.

On Friday, November 13th, the first party of ten volunteers left Dublin quietly as ordinary passengers from the North Wall on the *Lady Leinster*. Not until the following morning, when a newspaper report of their departure appeared, was it realised generally that the Irish Brigade was an accomplished fact, and that the advance guard had left Ireland.

The little advance guard consisted of:

Diarmuid O'Sullivan, a native of Killarney and son of Diarmuid O'Duibhne, well known in Gaelic League circles. Young Diarmuid, when a mere boy, served in the Easter Week rising under his idol, young Seán Heuston, who was afterwards executed. Later he joined the Dublin Brigade of the Irish Republican Army, and was at once selected for the active service unit. He was arrested and sentenced to death, but as he was then only seventeen years of age the sentence was commuted to penal servitude for life. Released from Dartmoor after the signing of the

Treaty, he joined the National Army, where he reached the rank of Commandant. The Military Governor of the province of Cáceres, speaking to me of Diarmuid O'Sullivan, described him as one of the smartest officers in Spain. He was second in command of the Irish bandera, and when Major Dalton, because of serious illness, was forced to return to Ireland, Capt. O'Sullivan automatically took charge.

Then there was P. J. Gallagher, member of the Sligo Corporation, who at an early age joined the Fianna, and later the National Army. He proved himself a loyal and brave officer. James Finnerty, Dublin, formerly in the I.R.A., suffered imprisonment in Dublin Castle and Arbour Hill. In the National Army he was Battalion Quartermaster. He was appointed Quartermaster to the bandera and carried out his responsible and difficult duties most satisfactorily.

Thomas Carew, Cashel, whose father was a Fenian and Sinn Féin pioneer. For I.R.A. activities he suffered terms of imprisonment, and was served with a deportation order to leave Ireland. He held the rank of Colonel in the National Army. John F. McCarthy, Co. Cork, had a fine I.R.A. record, and was wounded in action while leading an I.R.A. attack. He laid service in the National Army and in the Civic Guard.

David Tormey, Co. Westmeath, had been a member of the Westmeath flying column of the I.R.A., and, in 1921, was interned. After the Treaty he joined the National Army, and reached the rank of Captain. On resignation he joined the Civic Guard, from which he resigned to go to Spain with the Brigade, in which he was a First Lieutenant. Sean B. Murphy, Co. Cork, had been closely associated with the Irish language and other national organisations, and one of the pioneers of the Irish Corporate movement.

Others in this group of volunteers were John C. Muldoon, Navan, who had been one of the first to offer his services to the Irish Brigade; Bernard J. Connolly, solicitor, Longford, son of a former Deputy for Co. Longford, and Seán Garrahan,

Co. Longford, formerly a divisional engineer in the I.R.A., and later Captain in the National Army.

At Liverpool the party was joined by Dr. Freeman, son of a former Dublin police officer, and sailed the same evening for Lisbon.

A week later a second, and larger, party, with which I travelled, left Dublin by the same route. This group included the following volunteers, who were afterwards appointed officers:

Patrick Dalton, Dublin, a prominent I.R.A. leader, and former Colonel in the National Army, who was appointed Major in command of the bandera; Tom Hyde, Co. Cork, former National Army Captain and a member of the active service unit of the First Cork Brigade. He was killed in action on the Jarama front on 19th February. Padraig Quinn, Co. Kilkenny, former National Army Commandant, who had joined the I.R.A. at the age of sixteen, and in Spain was a Company Commander, and later second in command of the bandera.

Thomas Gunning, Co. Leitrim, who was my private secretary in Spain, with rank of Captain, Seán Cunningham, Belfast, former Commandant, National Army, and previously an I.R.A., Captain, who was in command of the bandera's machine-gun company. Tom O'Riordan, Co. Cork, former National Army officer, and an outstanding figure in the Anglo-Irish war.

Tom F. Smith, B.E., Dublin, who commanded "B" Company of the bandera; Edward Murphy, Co. Wicklow, a former National Army officer, who was bandera Adjutant; Michael Cagney, son of Dr. Cagney, Cork, one of the first to volunteer, who was an officer in the machine-gun company. Denis Kelly, Co. Roscommon, son of a prominent member of public boards in Co. Roscommon, who was imprisoned for Land League activities; George Timlin, Dublin, well known in sporting circles, who served in the National Army. James Clancy, Tipperary, with I.R.A. and long National Army service; Peter Lawlor of Kildare, and Dr. Peter O'Higgins, who was the bandera medical officer.

This party being of larger dimensions our departure from Dublin attracted more attention, and many gathered on the quay side to give us a send off. At Liverpool, before leaving by the *Avoceta* on the long sea trip to Lisbon, we took farewell of a large crowd, including Rev. S. Gillan, an Irish priest in Liverpool, who took a keen interest in the Irish Brigade and rendered invaluable assistance to the various groups passing through. There are many Irishmen in the Liverpool police, and these were as obliging as they were interested.

With our national flag, the tricolour, we carried the official flag of the Brigade—a red cross on a field of emerald green, bearing the inscription *In Hoc Signo Vinces*, from the banners of the brigades of former days.

We had the ship almost to ourselves, for there were not more than a dozen other passengers. A daily timetable was drawn up and every moment was occupied. Captain Gunning taught two Spanish classes daily, we had military lectures, deck games, whist drives and an Irish *ceilidhe* each night organised by Tom Casserly of Dublin. The captain and staff and the other passengers entered into the Irish atmosphere of the ship and altogether we had a very happy journey indeed. I presented the captain with my Irish blackthorn as a souvenir of the trip. The purser, Mr. Cochrane of Tyrone, and the wireless operator, Mr. Wright of Donnybrook, Dublin, left nothing undone to make our trip enjoyable.

At Lisbon we found all the Irish in the city and many Portuguese had assembled at the docks led by three Irish Dominican Fathers from Corpo Santo—Rev. Paul O'Sullivan, Rev. E. McVeigh, Rev. Joseph Dowdall—and Fr. Crowley, of the English College, Lisbon. The volunteers made a tour of the city, the priests, students and other Irish friends acting as guides. All returned to the ship for roll call at 10 p.m., where we remained overnight, and early next morning we attended Mass at the altar of St. Patrick in the Irish National church.

After Mass we visited the Irish convent of Bon Successo, and the Lumiar Relic of St. Brigid. The Mother Prioress sent hundreds of Rosary beads, Scapulars, Agnus Deis, Medals and Prayer Books to the brigade at Christmas. We also visited the English College, where we were most cordially received by Rev. J. J. Crowley, D.Ph. Then, after lunch on the *Avoceta* as guests of the captain, we set out on our long journey across Portugal to the Spanish frontier on luxurious buses supplied by General Franco's Minister in Lisbon—Señor Mariano Amoedo. It was well after midnight when the "all clear" was sounded by the Portuguese authorities at Elvas. In a few minutes we halted again, and the volunteers had the thrill of setting their feet on Spanish soil for the first time. Continuing to the city of Badajoz, we were there received by the Military Governor and his staff, and after partaking of their first Spanish meal the volunteers retired for the night.

All were astir early next morning. The volunteers entrained for Cáceres, which was to be the headquarters of the Irish Brigade. I handed over my charge to Major Dalton, and left the same evening for Dublin to continue arrangements for further groups of volunteers to complete the first Irish bandera.

I got through the Spanish, French, British, and Irish controls and was home in record time. I met the keymen and arranged for further groups via Liverpool and Lisbon, and discussed the probability of a special ship from an Irish port. After three busy days in Dublin I set off again for Cáceres in my anxiety that the volunteers already there should be getting through their training expeditiously.

In London I called to see La Cierva about a ship. He was to pay a flying visit to Hamburg next morning and suggested that I should accompany him, as he was returning to London at once and would then come with me to Spain. I agreed. Next morning we considered the possibility of delay in Hamburg, and as my immediate return to Spain was necessary we altered our plans. I set out for Cáceres alone, and La Cierva took a Dutch airliner for Amsterdam.

A few minutes after leaving Croydon the plane crashed in a fog. Fourteen died in the flames, including my friend. That great patriot and loyal friend died for his country as certainly as if an enemy bullet had found him on the Madrid front.

It was tragic irony that one of the greatest men in aviation, the inventor of the well-known auto-giro, should so meet his death in the prime of manhood.

But for some almost incredibly good police work I would have been unable to complete the journey. In my rush across Paris to catch the night mail at the Quai d'Orsay I left the attaché case containing my ticket, passport and some papers in the taxi. When the taxi was gone I discovered my loss, and the train was then due to leave in twenty minutes.

I had only one clue for the vital pursuit. On my leaving the taxi outside the station, another person had engaged it, saying *Gare du Nord*. I told a gendarme hurriedly and gave him my name. In the twinkling of an eye he was off by car.

I was very upset. I could get a new ticket, but the passport was essential. Without it I would have to return to Ireland. The train was due to leave in two minutes when the gendarme rushed on to the platform with the case. I had only time for swift thanks to which he replied, smiling broadly, *"Espagne, mon Général? Bon voyage!"* He had done splendid police work, considering the many thousands of taxis in Paris and their average speed. Evidently he knew the route that taxis take from Quai d'Orsay to Gare du Nord station—some miles apart.

At the outskirts of Salamanca my car was stopped by the Civil Guards, and there was a curt order to turn off the lights. The city was being bombarded by a fleet of Red planes, the anti-aircraft guns were in action, the place was in complete darkness and the streets deserted. There was only one casualty in the raid—a porter at the railway station, and when after a few minutes the raiders disappeared the city soon resumed its normal aspect. I left next morning for our headquarters at Cáceres.

Interest in the Irish Brigade was now growing fast, and when, on November 27th, a third and still larger party of volunteers—eighty-four in all—left for Liverpool and Lisbon, thousands gathered at the North Wall and each man was cheered as he walked up the gangway. Before leaving, the volunteers were presented with Rosaries, Agnus Deis and other religious emblems, the gift of the Right Rev. Monsignor Byrne, Clonmel, Dean of Waterford.

Seventeen counties were represented in this party, the largest contingent coming from Tipperary. Referring to their departure, the Right Rev. Monsignor Ryan, Dean of the Archdiocese of Cashel, preaching after Mass the following Sunday, said: "They have gone to fight the battle of Christianity against Communism. There are hosts of difficulties facing the men whom General O'Duffy is leading, and only heroes can fight such a battle. Those at home can help the cause with their prayers. The Rosary is more powerful than weapons of war. In the presence of Our Lord Jesus Christ let us promise that we will offer one decade of the family Rosary daily for poor suffering Spain; for the Irish boys who have gone out to fight the desperate battle that is threatening desolation all over the world. Let us pray that the destruction of civilisation may be averted, that Christ may live and reign, and that Communism and the power of Satan on earth may be brought to naught."

At Liverpool this party was joined on the *Aguila* by a number of young Irishmen from London and Manchester, and again a large crowd assembled at the quay.

Those who travelled on this occasion included Rev. J. Mulrean, chaplain, and the following volunteers who became officers:

Charles Horgan, Cork, who has had a splendid record in the I.R.A. and National Army; Thomas Cahill, Tipperary, who was an active member of the Irish Volunteers and underwent a hunger strike with me in Belfast Gaol, was a Captain in the National Army and later joined the Garda Síochána; and Eamon Horan,

U.D.C., Tralee, who had long service in the I.R.A. and National Army.

The departure of volunteers became a regular Friday feature, as parties had left on three consecutive Fridays, so again on the 4th December a big crowd assembled on the Dublin quays to wish God-speed to an expected contingent. They were disappointed however, as more elaborate plans were in mind for the next weekend, when the fourth and largest party, over a hundred, set sail. They arrived in Dublin carrying Papal, National and Spanish flags and wearing Sacred Heart badges sent from various Irish convents.

While Saturday's report of the departure of the fourth contingent from Dublin was being read in the newspapers, young men from every county in Ireland were moving westward to embark on a special ship from Galway Bay. Close on five hundred left Galway under cover of darkness in the small hours of Sunday morning to board a ship specially chartered to sail direct to Spain. Soon after this contingent had left Galway Pier in a tender, many more volunteers arrived only to find they had missed the boat. They returned in buses to their homes hoping to sail at a later date.

So secret were the arrangements kept that only those directly concerned knew of the departure until the last moment. It is related that Galway hotel proprietors were startled when they were knocked up at 1 a.m. and looking out on Eyre Square, the chief thoroughfare of Galway, found it blocked by buses and hundreds of private cars. Only a few minutes before, the spacious square had been deserted. Quickly the hotels were thrown open and after short meals the unexpected visitors left again to board their buses and cars. This time the entire fleet of vehicles made in the direction of the pier. Within a few minutes the tender *Dun Aengus*, which had been under steam for over an hour, threw open her gangways.

It was only then that those citizens of Galway who had left their beds to investigate the mystery of this strange invasion learned that they were witnessing the first departure for Spain of a draft of the Irish Brigade on a large all-Ireland scale. The volunteers hurried aboard the *Dun Aengus*, while on the pier and the surrounding thoroughfare now black with people, young women and old wiped tears from their eyes to smile at departing brothers, husbands, sons and sweethearts.

The *Dun Aengus* drew off from the pier with three shrill blasts on her siren at 2:15 a.m. Then, as handkerchiefs waved and voices from the darkness were raised in farewell, somebody on the pier began singing "Faith of Our Fathers." A thousand voices took up the hymn. From the tender there floated back to the pier that solemn strain. Then the "Soldier's Song" which reechoed back more faintly from the receding tender.

Amongst those on the quayside to see the men off were Rev. T. Fahy, Professor, University College, Galway, and Rev. J. O'Donohoe, C.C., Galway.

Swiftly the lights of the *Dun Aengus* retreated into the blackness of the harbour, soon to be lost to the sight of those remaining behind, and then the stillness was broken by the roar of all types of motor engines as the buses and cars swept through Galway again, making homeward to Cork, Dublin, Belfast, Clonmel, various towns in Kerry, Limerick, Wexford and other parts of the country.

When the tender had got out in the bay, the wind rose and there were squalls of heavy rain. The men on the unsheltered upper deck were soon wet through, and those below began to suffer from seasickness. On the whole they bore the hardness of their lot cheerfully, especially those on the open deck, who, although drenched through and shivering with the intense cold, never murmured.

At about 5:30 a.m., when no sign of the ship had been seen, Captain Goggins, of the *Dun Aengus*, decided there was no use in further cruising around, and the tender was hove to in a more sheltered position to await daylight. For a couple of hours there was silence aboard the little vessel, except for the steady tramping backwards and forwards of the men on deck, who kept up a ceaseless patrol, looking for the vessel that was to bring them forth on their great adventure.

Dawn broke with the wind rising and the rain coming in sleety squalls. Before night had fully cleared away, all who could get on deck turned their eyes seawards in eager search for what all were calling "the mystery ship". There was no sign of her however, and hearts sank again. Doubt as to whether their adventure would ever materialise began to enter even the stoutest hearts, and there was talk of putting back to Galway.

The *Dun Aengus* again put out towards the open sea and no sooner had she rounded Black Head than a large vessel was sighted steaming close in to the shore. The *Dun Aengus* immediately swung about and guided her further back into the bay. It was almost 11 a.m. before the big ship and the little one came alongside each other. Then there was the troublesome task of making them fast in the rising gale, but at last this was accomplished, and the two vessels were fast moored to each other.

Rope ladders were let down the side of the bigger vessel, and the volunteers forgot their coldness as the spirit of their great undertaking again flared up in them. Soon they were scrambling actively up the ladders, carrying their attaché cases and other belongings. Dixies, full of hot soup, were awaiting them, and when they had taken this they were hurried below, where arrangements had already been made for them. As only one man at a time could climb up the swaying rope ladder, and as the vessels were swinging heavily in the gale, transhipment was a lengthy and dangerous task, but was completed safely about 3 p.m.

Some thirty-five of the men now re-embarked on the *Dun Aengus*, leaving nearly five hundred of their comrades aboard. The lines were cast off, the little vessel's hooter blew three times as a salute from the men aboard her to their gallant comrades, and then she steamed back to Galway.

The gale continued during the greater part of the troopship's journey to Ferrol, a Spanish seaport, and the volunteers endured much further hardship *en route*. On reaching Ferrol Bay they were transferred for the night to the *Domino*, the ship on which La Cierva had intended the brigade should travel. Here they enjoyed their first comfortable night's rest and the first good meal since leaving their homes almost a week before.

Next morning they entrained on a twenty-four-hour journey to Salamanca. There they had a great reception, were met by military bands and marched through the streets to the City Hall, where dinner awaited them. They were welcomed by the Mayor, high military and church authorities, and many of the principal citizens. After enjoying generous hospitality the volunteers entrained on the last lap of the journey to their headquarters at Cáceres. The Military Governor, Civil Governor, Mayor, Judges, other leading citizens and their Irish comrades who had previously reached there awaited the arrival of the train. Every house in the city was decorated in honour of the brigade, and although the volunteers were almost worn out from the effects of the journey they were constrained to march through the streets so that the waiting thousands who lined the route to welcome them to Cáceres might not be disappointed.

The departure of the men from Galway, while attended by many discomforts, was a successful achievement. The seven hundred volunteers who travelled to Passage East on the night of January 6th would, I believe, gladly have suffered even worse if they had met with the same success. Instead they suffered intense disappointment from the non-arrival of the ship which was to take them to Spain.

Early in the morning of January 7th a ship was to arrive at Passage East, a fishing village seven miles from Waterford City. Throughout the night the quiet country roads were lighted by beams of motor car lights, and at midnight the little village of some fifty houses was thronged with men. Unlike Galway, Passage East seemed more or less to expect them. All roads leading to Waterford were patrolled by the Guards, all cars were stopped, the numbers taken and the drivers asked for their licences. In some cases they were questioned as to where they were going and whence they were coming.

The time of their ship's arrival was not known to the men, and as the hours rolled by they remained in high spirits, and paraded the streets singing popular songs to the strains of bagpipes. They continuously scanned the river mouth for sign of the lights of a ship, the villagers joining in the eager watch. The local people, though most hospitable, had not the means to cater for such an influx of visitors and soon all available refreshments were gone.

That January day broke bright and sunny, and the volunteers continued their watch cheerfully enough. When a coal boat came slowly up the river they rushed to the pier only to find their hopes frustrated. Hungry and tired they were greatly chagrined when told at about 11 a.m. that the ship was not coming. They remained hopeful until the transport had actually arrived to bring them back to their homes after their all-night vigil, and manfully expressed their willingness to spend even another night under the same conditions, if they could get to their comrades in Spain.

The people of Passage East felt the disappointment almost as keenly as the volunteers themselves and their kindness and hospitality on the occasion will not soon be forgotten.

In Spain the military authorities had made all preparations for the reception of this contingent which was to form the second or reserve bandera of the Irish Brigade. I was afterwards informed that the ship was commandeered hurriedly by the navy for service at Málaga on the day it was to leave for Ireland. The Admiral in charge of the zone apparently was not in a position at the time to notify general headquarters at Salamanca. Such are the exigencies of war.

THE BRIGADE WHILE IN TRAINING

IMMEDIATELY the main body of the Irish Brigade arrived at our headquarters in Cáceres, and when we were allotted our permanent quarters in the barracks a course of intensive training began. We had in our ranks many who had been through the Great War, and many who had seen service in the Irish Republican and National armies. For these the course was more in the nature of a refresher, and they were quick to acquaint themselves with the latest methods of warfare. Our junior volunteers—many not out of their teens—took kindly to the training, were even keener than their elders and never seemed to tire.

General Franco directed that one of the best instructors in his army, Captain Capablanca, should take charge of the training of the Irish unit. Every bandera in turn received the finishing touches from the Captain, who was not only a first-class instructor, but had a splendid fighting record. The only drawback was that he did not speak a word of English. This necessitated bringing in a number of young Spanish officers and sergeants who had a knowledge of English. These too worked very hard and effectively.

The Tercio comprises the cream of the Spanish army—the best fighters, the best trained and best disciplined soldiers, and its battle cry is "Long live death." The founder of the Tercio is

General Millán-Astray, who, on his retirement with a multiplicity of wounds, was succeeded in command by Colonel, now General Franco. The leader, while the Irish brigade was in Spain, was Colonel Yague.

We regarded it therefore as a very great privilege to be admitted as a distinct unit of the Tercio—the fifteenth bandera—and we were the first foreigners to be so signally honoured.

The Spanish system of military drill and ceremonial is very different to ours, and while we were allowed the option of continuing our own system, we considered it desirable from many points of view to adapt ourselves gradually to the Tercio system. When we had selected our officers, Captain Capablanca took two classes each day, sergeants and N.C.O.'s being instructed simultaneously. In Spain sergeants are not referred to as non-commissioned officers. They have much more responsibility than in other armies, are saluted by all subordinate ranks, and are better paid than junior officers. A sergeant commands a platoon, which consists of three squads—two rifle squads and a light machine-gun squad, each in charge of an N.C.O., which means a corporal. Two platoons form a section, and there are three sections in the company, each commanded by a lieutenant. There is in addition a trench mortar platoon attached to each company, which is commanded by a sub-lieutenant or sergeant-major, the whole embracing two hundred and three all ranks and being commanded by a captain. A bandera consists of four companies—three rifle companies, and a machine-gun company consisting of one hundred and thirty-eight all ranks, and is commanded by a major.

Captain Capablanca had prepared a series of twelve booklets, which were translated into English and dealt with the duties of officers, sergeants and N.C.O.'s, drill, musketry, sub-machine-guns, battle formation, offensive and defensive tactics. Training in the barrack rooms, on the barrack square, on the ranges, practice in bomb throwing, route marches, skirmishing, tank warfare, and so on, continued strenuously from November until the middle of February, when the bandera was moved to the front lines. Considering the brief period of training given to the Spanish soldiers themselves, and the training of Kitchener's army before it set out for Flanders, the Irish Brigade was afforded in comparison, very good opportunities under the circumstances.

From the arrival of the first Irish volunteer until we left his command the Military Governor of Cáceres, his Excellency Colonel de Pinillos, was unremitting in his attention to the Brigade. He allotted us the best quarters in the Central Military Barracks. A very busy man, with big responsibilities, not only as Military Governor of the city, but as Franco's representative for the huge Province of Cáceres, and Officer Commanding the troops therein, he yet found time to give his personal attention to our many requests. Nothing seemed to him too good for the fifteenth bandera, and we regarded him as our kindly host. At the various religious and social functions he gave our officers pride of place. He attended Mass with us Sunday after Sunday, and after Mass invariably waited in the Plaza to take the salute as the bandera marched past. He was also responsible for having Ireland's national flag displayed with the Spanish flag in every town in the province, and the military bands in his area were instructed to learn and play our national anthem. A remarkable honour was conferred by him with the approval of the Bishop of Cáceres—our national anthem was played at the Consecration by the Spanish military bands and later by our own.

The reverence of the Irish troops during the various religious services, their attendance in such large numbers at daily Mass, their visits to the churches at night were a revelation to the other troops in Cáceres. The Bishop himself was so much impressed that he missed few, if any, of our ceremonies.

The priests of the diocese are very poor indeed, finding it hard to get the bare necessities of life. This fact came to the knowledge of the volunteers and they made a collection among themselves on the Sunday before we left for the front. I was handed a sum of one thousand five hundred pesetas (£30) to be presented to the Bishop "for his priests in appreciation of the kindly and paternal interest which his Lordship the Bishop graciously bestowed on us during our stay in Cáceres".

The bandera flag was an Irish wolfhound in saffron on a ground of emerald green, and in addition the four companies had each a pennant representing one of the four Irish provinces. By permission these flags were unfurled in the sanctuary during all church services, with a special guard of honour.

We were permitted to wear the Irish harp emblem on each lapel of the tunic. Enterprising firms in Cáceres and neighbouring cities soon had the harp emblems in gold, silver and bronze in their shop windows, and found a ready sale among the señoritas and youths, with all of whom the Irishmen were very popular. Handkerchiefs and ties with the harp embroidered thereon were also on sale.

The food in Spain is very much like the food in Ireland, the only difference being in the manner of cooking and serving. Two pesetas per day is deducted from the pay of each soldier to cover cost of food, and a daily balance sheet is produced. There was not much difficulty in procuring meat, bacon, fowl, potatoes and other vegetables, rice, coffee or bread while in training. With the two pesetas, which worked out at about ten pence in our money, our Quartermaster was able to provide very good fare. He went to the markets himself with an interpreter, purchased our requirements, brought the food to barracks and handed it over to Irish cooks.

A special tribute is due to our cooks. I was quartered in the principal hotel in Cáceres, but the only meals I really enjoyed were those cooked and served by our own volunteers—splendid soup, real Irish stew, nicely-boiled potatoes, and all free from olive oil. It is not possible to get a meal in any hotel in Spain without the meat, fish, fowl, vegetables, in fact everything, swimming in olive oil. It serves no purpose to complain to the waiter. To him and to every Spaniard olive oil is regarded as an essential.

There is no such thing as tea in Spain as we understand it. Only green tea is served, and we did not take kindly to it. Even if you supply your own tea to the Spanish cook it is served cold and weak in a beer glass, and always without sugar or milk. The coffee, however, is quite good, and if you want a beverage you simply must develop a taste for it.

Irish stew was our favourite dish and because of the demand for it there was lack of variety, but majority rule prevailed. The rice was good and wholesome, and in the cooking of this the Spanish cooks excelled. The bread, when a little stale, was very sustaining. Bacon or ham is usually eaten raw in Spain—although it is supposed to be smoked. Eggs are not usually served in the shell. If you ask for boiled eggs they are simply put in a bowl of hot water and brought to the table. There is a sweet course, chiefly confectionery, and not at all digestible.

An old Spanish custom into which the Irishmen rarely fell was that of the *siesta*. Luncheon or dinner takes, as a rule, over two hours, as it is the custom to have long intervals between the six or eight courses. Personally I considered this a great waste of time, for it is no exaggeration to say that nearly half the day is usually spent between eating and the mid-day *siesta* that follows a long and heavy meal. For myself, during a period of nine months, I did not take half a dozen meals in the dining-room. I had the food brought to my office and finished it off in about ten minutes. The few Irishmen who had their food in hotels, however, soon developed the unhurried Spanish manner of dining.

The Spaniards can spend hours at a stretch in a cafe over a cup of coffee or sipping a single glass of light beer. They are a very sober people, and in the army especially it is considered an unpardonable offence to get drunk. During my time in Spain I never saw a citizen or soldier suffering from the effects of alcohol.

The favourite drinks of the Irish brigade were light Spanish beer, vino, and coffee. The beer was rather dear, vino was very cheap, but quickly intoxicated, and coffee prevailed. Whatever the drink, our lads consumed it without delay, and left the cafe, a custom the inhabitants could not understand at all. I am proud to say that I did not observe one member of the Brigade under the influence of drink at any time, and I was in close touch with all ranks.

After about a month in Spain the Brigade was provided with a uniform of sorts—very poor material and very badly fitting indeed—but the only thing that could be procured. As I mentioned previously the textiles and the factories were in the hands of the enemy. Notwithstanding this the Irishmen, because of their erect bearing and fine physique, to me looked smarter on parade than any other soldiers in Spain. The uniform was not replaced during our period of service, and after ten weeks in the trenches, worn night and day, it was threadbare—in rags. Yet the volunteers bore with it, and though they were feeling ashamed, there was no complaint or loss of *morale*.

Parcels and letters from Ireland were often held up *en route* for weeks, and many never were received. If there was one grievance it was this. A letter, a newspaper, a packet of cigarettes, or razor blades was always a God-send. Apart from the intrinsic value, it showed that the Brigade was not forgotten in the homeland. I found it necessary to send an officer weekly to Lisbon, and often he returned empty-handed.

When we had about six weeks without any parcels and only a few letters I travelled to Lisbon myself to investigate the position. I was told there was nothing for the Brigade, and thereupon requested permission to go myself through the customs sheds at the port. After many preliminaries—going from one high customs official to a still higher—my request was granted. It was a formidable task, for there were twenty large sheds packed with boxes, hampers and trunks, all piled on one another. The officer in charge tried to convince me that I was wasting my time, but was kind enough to detail a few hefty and obliging porters to make a search.

After half an hour I found one large hamper addressed to the Brigade, and after this discovery everything was easy. Every shed was visited, every label scrutinised. We completed the job in about two hours, collecting two lorry loads of letters, news-papers and parcels. The Portuguese revenue authorities were entitled to the fees on dutiable goods collected by the addressee at Lisbon—although the destination was Spain. We overcame this difficulty after consultation with the Chief of Police, who agreed to send a police escort to the Spanish frontier to ensure the hampers would not be opened in Portugal. General Franco's Minister in Lisbon looked after the transport across Portugal.

The international observers at the Spanish border had then to be satisfied that the hampers did not contain warlike materi-als. The frontier having been successfully negotiated, further dif-ficulties arose—transport to brigade headquarters at Cáceres. The one railway line was used exclusively for the transport of troops; lorries and cars were all commandeered. Again the Mil-itary Governor of Cáceres came to my aid.

I arrived in Cáceres late at night with my precious cargo. My mission to Lisbon was known to every man in the Brigade and they were full of expectancy. I suspended training next day, the lorries were unloaded in the Irish lines and the men lined up in a hollow square. Every man received a letter, a newspaper or a parcel and many had a dozen letters—the arrears of several weeks—all handed by me personally to each man. It was a happy day for many, but a few volunteers were sad. Three received news of the death of their mothers, others of the death of friends.

The Brigade owes much to Father McVeigh, O.P., of the Irish Church, Lisbon, through whose hands the letters to and from Ireland passed, and who cheerfully gave his time and energy to this work while the Brigade was in Spain.

I was accompanied to Lisbon by Lieutenant Matemores, a young officer of the Spanish Air Force, whose mother was Irish. He was a great pilot and a fearless fighter. Early in the war his plane was shot down by enemy anti-aircraft guns, when he was bombing a Red stronghold near Merida. He was made prisoner, and was so seriously wounded that his gaolers thought he would not attempt to escape. He did escape, however, and while convalescent was attached to the Irish Brigade, in which he was most popular.

Special mention should be made of the splendid service rendered by Miss Gertrude Gaffney, the Dublin journalist. Her articles on the Brigade were eagerly read in Spain and brought comfort to many an anxious Irish parent at home. Miss Gaffney, not content with writing, opened a fund to provide comforts, and every volunteer had something from the huge hamper she forwarded, and which I opened on the barrack square in the presence of the assembled Brigade.

All got cigarettes, all got a couple of pairs of socks, but when it came to distribute cardigans and shirts I was confronted with a difficulty. There were hundreds of these, but not sufficient to give one to each. The only solution was to hold a raffle, tickets a peseta each (the officers generously purchasing tickets for their men)—the proceeds to be devoted to the Brigade dependents' fund.

The Sunday evening concerts in the dining hall were eagerly looked forward to. There was never an absentee, the concerts were thoroughly enjoyable and the standard reached in singing, dancing, recitation and instrumental music surprised the Spanish officers in Cáceres, who never missed one of these entertainments.

Many volunteers looked forward to seeing a bull-fight, and a special performance was arranged for us. The toreadors were dressed in green, and the darts used to infuriate the bulls were bedecked with the Irish national colours. The matador (the killer) dedicated the bull to Ireland, by saluting in front of the Irish box before the fight, and by presenting one of the animal's ears to an Irishman after the fight.

It was evident from the outset that this form of pastime did not appeal to the Irishmen's sense of sportsmanship. Many left after the first fight and I think few, if any, attended subsequent performances. Their sympathy was all with the unfortunate animal, and as he romped round among his many torturers, he was voted the best sport on the field.

When the volunteers returned to their barracks for tea, a unanimous wish was expressed that Franco would abolish bull-fighting as a national pastime in the new Spain.

There was no politics in the Irish Brigade. It was made appear in Ireland that the majority were either blue shirts, or green shirts of the Corporate Party. The facts are that only a small proportion ever belonged to any organisation, and in the selection of officers and N.C.O.'s scrupulous care was taken to avoid any distinction in this regard. I believe that from the day we left Dublin until the day we returned there was not one political discussion. For the vast majority of the volunteers the greatness of the cause for which they endured so much made party politics seem very petty. Of course, the Irish newspapers were eagerly read in Spain and where it was reported that individuals of whatever party made disparaging remarks about the Brigade it was circulated like wildfire. The men were very proud, and very sensitive of slight.

To emphasise the non-political character of the Brigade I sent home the following statement for publication:

"It might appear from some speeches made in Ireland recently that the Irish Brigade would be prepared to take advantage of the sacrifices of men like the late Tom Hyde, Gabriel Lee, and the Tralee martyrs to further the ends of some political party. The only organisation in which I was interested was the National Corporate Party, and I announced in the public press before I left Ireland that the activities of that organisation were suspended. I wish to state now that should I return to Ireland, as, please God, I shall, it is not my intention to take any part in politics directly or indirectly.

"We did not come here to further the interests of any political party, be it Fianna Fáil, Fine Gael, Labour or the National Corporate Party. Some may be disappointed at this statement, but as the leader of our brave Irish boys in Spain, I would be false to the trust they have placed in me, were I to entertain any political ambitions. I shall never exploit their sacrifices. There is no politics in this Brigade—all are now united under one banner—the banner of Christ the King against Communism."

Cáceres, the biggest medical centre in Spain, has five large military hospitals. Here are the medical headquarters of the Tercio, of the Moorish troops, the Felange have an hospital here also, and in the Central Military Hospital two wards were assigned for the Irish Brigade.

On Christmas Eve I was requested by the Military Governor to make a tour of the hospitals and was privileged to present a Christmas gift to each patient personally. During the tour, which occupied over four hours, I was deeply impressed by the spirit of the wounded. Some were beyond recovery, many had lost limbs, others were suffering intense pain, but all appeared cheerful. A little concert was staged in each hospital after the presentation of gifts, and a military band played the Irish national anthem. Miss Aileen O'Brien, of Dublin, accompanied me and interpreted for the patients.

On Christmas morning there was a full parade to the church of San Domingo, where Father Mulrean said three Masses, followed by Benediction. Afterwards the Bishop of the diocese, the Military Governor and his staff, the Mayor and Corporation, the Civil Governor, the Judges of the Military Courts, the Chief of Police, and the chief officers of the Requetes and Felange visited my quarters to convey their Christmas greetings through me to the Brigade. At twelve noon the Military Governor conveyed to me the following message addressed to him from General Franco:

"I beg you to express in my name, Christmas greetings to all ranks of the Irish bandera and my best wishes for their happiness and success. Having had knowledge that General

O'Duffy visited the various hospitals yesterday and distributed presents to the wounded soldiers, say to the General that I am grateful for his act of kindness and assistance, and greet him most affectionately in my name."

The chief of the Tercio (Legion) wired:

"The whole corps of officers, sub-officers and N.C.O.'s and all the soldiers of the legion greet the General and all his men, wishing them days of glory in the valiant crusade. Long live Ireland. Long live Spain."

The following message was received from the Very Rev. Paul O'Sullivan, O.P., Rector of the Irish Church in Lisbon:

"I send to you and your heroic volunteers my most hearty Christmas greetings. All the Irish Fathers in Corpo Santo, and the Mother Prioress and the Irish Nuns in Bon Successo join with me in this message. We are faithfully keeping our promise to remember you in every one of our daily Masses. With all my heart and soul I pray God bless you, and He will bless you."

Amongst the many messages received from Ireland was a greeting from the Lord Mayor of Dublin, Alderman Alfred Byrne, T.D.

On behalf of the Brigade I sent the following Christmas message to Ireland:

"Our first bandera has taken shape, and the hopes and dreams of our gallant young Irishmen are now a living reality. All the men are well and fit and happy, and without fear for the future. The men's families and friends can rest assured that here, in sunny Cáceres, we will have an Irish Christmas, with the spirit of the great Feast in our hearts. Our thoughts are with you today, as we know yours are with us."

The volunteers had a special Christmas dinner, after which a most enjoyable concert was held in the dining room. I conveyed to them the above messages, which I acknowledged in their name.

Although a bit homesick they were in great form, jubilant and happy. One and all assured me that their Christmas in Spain was the most enjoyable they ever had.

On New Year's Eve, at midnight, Colonel Yague, chief of the Tercio, and about forty Spanish officers paid a surprise visit to my quarters for an impromptu at-home. A few minutes afterwards the Irish officers, who were evidently "in the know", arrived, and there was a very happy exchange of felicitations. Again, on New Year's Day, greetings were received from the Generalissimo, and the various arms of the service. The day was marked by our first church parade in uniform.

In Guadalupe is the great Franciscan monastery, which rises like a fortress from the centre of the town. Its treasures, the gifts of generations, are of almost fabulous value, and its galleries house some of the most precious masterpieces of the great Spanish artists. A determined drive was made in August, 1936, by eight thousand Red militia to capture the monastery and its treasures. The people of Guadalupe and the neighbouring villages gathered in the monastery to the number of six thousand, and with few arms and little food held the fortress until they were relieved by Franco's forces after a three weeks' siege. Even yet the enemy outposts are only a few miles from the town, which lies in a little neck of Franco's territory.

It was to this historic and sanctified spot the Military Governor led all the available officers of the Brigade on Sunday, 3rd January, 1937. At the various towns *en route*, Trujillo—the birthplace of Pizarro, who conquered Peru for Spain—at Lagrosan, and at Larita, the garrisons were drawn up awaiting our arrival, and we received in each town an official welcome from the civil authorities.

When we arrived in Guadalupe the town was *en fête*. Thousands of school children, collected from miles around, carried miniature Irish flags, little girls and boys presented flowers in green, white and orange, and when the garrison presented arms the military band played "The Wearing of the Green." We were met at the entrance to the town by the Prior of the monastery, and from every window the flag of Ireland waved side by side with the flag of Spain. Mass was celebrated in the beautiful monastery church and at the Consecration the Irish national anthem was played.

At lunch high tributes were paid to the Irish Brigade by the Prior, who referred to it as "the most gallant little band that ever left a nation's shores for a great ideal, seeking no reward in this world". After lunch we were shown the priceless vestments and tapestries of the monastery, and venerated its most famous treasure, the miraculous statue of Our Lady of Guadalupe.

The return journey to Cáceres was most remarkable. Along over sixty miles of country road, we passed through a veritable corridor of armed guards, posted in pairs at intervals of one hundred yards. From Guadalupe to Cáceres they stretched in one unbroken line—regular soldiers, Felange, Requetes, Civil Guards—all presenting arms as our little party passed by.

Similarly on every Sunday and feast day the Military Governor arranged for excursions to neighbouring towns, the local garrisons were turned out, the towns were gaily decorated and we were received by the Municipal and Church authorities. I heard afterwards that the Military Governor was very much concerned about my health, and considerately planned these little parties to take me away from my work, although in fact I worked no harder in Spain than at any time.

On 6th January, 1937, I left Cáceres on a hurried visit to Dublin to arrange for a second reserve bandera, to deal with financial matters, to arrange for a piper's band, etc.

The fall of Málaga was celebrated with great enthusiasm in Cáceres. A parade of all the troops in the province took place. High Mass was celebrated in the cathedral, the Bishop presiding, and the *Te Deum* was chanted in the church of San Maria.

Singular tributes were paid to Ireland on this occasion. Our ban-dera, under Captain O'Sullivan, headed the parade of which Major Dalton was given charge, and I was appointed reviewing officer. The ceremonies were under the auspices of the students of the Spanish Universities Felange.

On Ash Wednesday morning there was a parade to the church of San Domingo, where the blessed ashes were distrib-uted.

On 6th February the usual routine was proceeding in bar-racks when at noon a message was received that General Franco, who was on his way from Seville to Salamanca, would stop at Cáceres in the afternoon to inspect the Irish troops. There was jubilation in the Irish lines when the announcement was made.

At the appointed time the bandera paraded fully armed and equipped, with the Irish flag at its head. When the Generalis-simo's car entered the barracks the general salute was sounded, and a guard of honour, under Lieutenant Gallagher of Sligo, presented arms. As General Franco stepped from his car the bandera presented arms.

The Generalissimo passed along the entire line, pausing to salute and bow profoundly before the flag of Ireland. Then the bandera fell into marching order, and as each section marched past, the officers and men saluted in Spanish style, shouting wholeheartedly "*Viva Franco*," "*Viva España*," and "*Viva Irlanda*."

When the parade was dismissed General Franco warmly complimented Major Dalton on the appearance of both officers and men. The Military Governor presented the Irish officers individually to him, and the Generalissimo, in a short address, said:

"It is an honour and a great happiness to me to have met today the heroic Irish volunteers, and I wish to pay the highest tribute to the smart and martial bearing of the officers and men. With war conditions prevailing, and so many journeys to be made, I regret I could not give longer notice of my coming. The short notice only goes to prove the more how capable you are, and I look with joy and confidence to the day when you and your Spanish comrades will win new honours for your flag, fighting for the glory of Ireland, the glory of Spain, and the glory of our holy Faith." General Franco was cheered by the volunteers again and again as he was leaving.

On my return to Cáceres from Lisbon, where I had been looking after the delayed letters and parcels at the time of his visit, General Franco telephoned to me expressing his "supreme gratification" and complimenting me on the splendid appearance of the bandera. He asked me to convey again to all ranks his appreciation and compliments.

Chapter X

IRELAND'S DAY IN AN OLD SPANISH CITY

TO MARK the end of our training and our official farewell before leaving for the front, I unveiled, on Sunday, 31st January, 1937, a tablet commemorating our stay in Cáceres, in the church of Santo Domingo, which had been known as the "Irish" church since the first contingent's arrival. The tablet is of bronze and bears the shields of Ireland and of Spain on either side. At the top is a Celtic cross and at the foot a miniature of the Madonna and Child, shamrocks and Irish designs fill the corners. The inscription in Irish, Spanish and English, reads:

"To the glory of God and the honour of Ireland, in remembrance of the 15th Bandera, Irish Brigade, of the Tercio, which worshipped in this church while serving in the cause of the Faith, and of Ireland's ancient ally and protector, Spain."

The entire bandera, in full war kit, was present at the ceremony. The Bishop presided at the Mass, and afterwards gave Benediction of the Most Holy Sacrament. In the sanctuary were the Military Governor, the Civil Governor, the Mayor and other notabilities.

In seats in the nave were the Spanish and Irish officers, representatives of the public authorities of the city and province of Cáceres, and delegations from the Catholic organisations, while the body of the church was occupied by the Irish bandera and representatives of the armed forces of the Spanish State. The bandera choir sang the Mass and at the Consecration our anthem was played. Afterwards, during Benediction, the bandera sang "Faith of Our Fathers."

A guard of honour of Irish officers, led by Captain Diarmuid O'Sullivan, and consisting of Captains Quinn and Cunningham and Lieutenants Hyde and Clancy, led the procession from the altar to the Lady chapel, in which the tablet, still veiled by the flags of Ireland and Spain, was situated. A brief pause followed while the Bishop's procession came slowly through the dense throng and filed into position before the tablet. Then a sharp order rang out, and the entire bandera, which had been facing towards the high altar, turned right as one man.

Having saluted the Bishop, I unveiled the tablet, saying: "On behalf of the officers and men of the first bandera of the Irish Brigade, I unveil this tablet to the glory of God and the honour of Ireland." The flags fluttered apart, a steel-helmeted guard of honour of non-commissioned officers presented arms, and the band played the Irish anthem.

Major P. Dalton, officer commanding the bandera, handed me a silver casket with a Celtic cross engraved upon the lid. Within was more than 2,000 pesetas, an offering from the bandera to the Franciscan Fathers who had placed the church at our disposal during our stay in Cáceres. I presented the casket to the Father Guardian, thanking the Fathers for their kindness to the troops, I referred to the bonds between Spain and Ireland, dwelling on the fact that our common Faith, even more than ties of race and blood, bound the two peoples together.

"As Spain was to Ireland in her hour of need," I said, "so the Catholic people of Ireland wished to be to Spain today, and this tablet will be a reminder of the glory of the cause which brought us here."

The Military Governor responding, praised the spirit of the volunteers. "For many centuries," he said, "Spain had loved the Irish nation, and was bound to it by a common faith and by blood spilt together in a common cause. Today the pledges of centuries were renewed, and in a world which had almost forgotten the things of the spirit, the glorious example of Catholic Ireland and her brave sons, shone forth to give new courage to those who fought the old, old battle for Christ. Cáceres will be for ever honoured in the knowledge that the tradition of centuries had been perpetuated within her walls, and that she had been chosen as the first home of the new Crusaders from the beloved and heroic 'Green Isle of Erin'."

The Bishop then delivered an allocution, with many references to the work of Irish saints and missionaries. He dwelt especially on the intimate association with Ireland of his own Order, the Dominicans, and of the Franciscans, and of the colleges founded by Irish priests at Louvain, Lisbon, and elsewhere. The Bishop concluded with emotion: "And you, sons of St. Patrick, who have left your homes to help Spain to bear the cross which has so often been borne upon the shoulders of Ireland, by your example here today, and by your generous gifts to this church, but above all, by your fervent devotion during Mass and Benediction, have given every one of us who saw you, an example and a lesson on the meaning of the Catholic Faith."

The ceremony then ended with the Episcopal blessing, but all day the townspeople visited the church to inspect the *recuerdo de los soldados Irlandeses* (the gift of the Irish soldiers).

A parade through the city was arranged to allow the thousands who had been unable to enter the church an opportunity of seeing the first Irish bandera fully trained and equipped. After three days of incessant rain—practically the first rain we had experienced since we came to Caceros—we were blessed with a dry and sunny day. The men were in excellent form, fighting fit, and longing to stretch their legs after three days in barracks without their customary route marches.

A saluting base was fixed in the main square opposite the City Hall, from which the flag of Ireland flew side by side with that of Spain, and when I arrived to take the salute, accompanied by the Bishop, the Military Governor and his staff, and the

Mayor and Corporation, fully ten thousand people packed the square and the surrounding streets, houses and balconies.

There was an uproar of applause in the street newly named "The Alcázar" as the steel-helmeted advance guard of the bandera swung into view. Lieutenant Tom Hyde, later killed in action, bore our national flag. Flying high above the heads of the crowd it seemed to be uplifted upon a host of bayonets. Never, even at home, have I seen that tricolour given a more enthusiastic reception than when it headed the biggest parade which ever passed through the Plaza of Cáceres.

Major Dalton headed the parade, with Captain O'Sullivan, Captain Smith, Captain Quinn and Captain Cunningham leading their respective companies, followed by the field stretcher units. Tall, purposeful-looking men, marching in column of threes—the Tercio formation—the brigade made a gallant show, passing the saluting base with a precision which drew cheer after cheer from the spectators.

Behind the Irish column came detachments representing the Army, the Air Force, Civil Guards, Assault Guards, Felange and Carlists, all marching in full war equipment. With a fanfare of trumpets the end of a long procession finally passed, and with shouts of *Viva Irlanda* the crowds reluctantly dispersed.

After lunch the Spanish and Irish officers were the guests of the men at a concert in the barracks, at which a fine display of amateur talent was given. Two hours of songs, grave and gay, Irish music and recitation. At the interval I congratulated all ranks on their fine appearance on parade and gave them the latest news of Ireland, from which I had just returned. The silence was tense as I spoke of happenings in the homeland, but wild cheering broke out when I told of the thousands whose hearts and thoughts were with us in Spain, and of comrades who were only waiting an opportunity to come to fight by our side.

Before the end of the concert I received the following message from General Franco, which I read for the Brigade amid scenes of enthusiasm:

"I have just heard of the parade of the Irish bandera this morning and that it was received with great acclamation by the population of Cáceres. I fully appreciate the value of the enthusiasm which the Brigade has aroused in Spain, for which I communicate to you, General, my thanks and my affection."

The events concluded with a farewell reception which I gave to the Bishop, Military Governor, Mayor and civil authorities and the Spanish and Irish officers. The occasion was availed of by the officers and men of the Brigade to make a presentation to his Excellency Colonel Luis de Martin-Penillos, the Military Governor of the Province and City of Cáceres, as an appreciation of and token of affection for our best friend from the first day we arrived in Spain—a spontaneous act "to remind our kindly host of the first Irish bandera, whether we are fighting at the front, whether we have returned to Ireland, or whether we have found soldiers' graves fighting in Spain for the Faith of our fathers".

"No kindness could be too much," said the Military Governor in reply, "to show my gratitude and the gratitude of all true Spaniards to our Catholic comrades in arms, true sons of the Island of Saints. Ireland's heroism, her faith and her sacrifices, her gallantry, and devotion to ideals, have made her, though a small country, one of the greatest. Illustrious sons of her soil, and their descendants, have time and again captained the victorious armies of Spain throughout the world—such Generals as O'Donnell, O'Shea, and O'Reilly. Spain will never forget these names, and dearest in her heart will be the gallant Irish volunteers who came to her today, hoping for no honour but the honour of serving God, and at the same time helping an ancient friend of Ireland."

So ended Ireland's day as the midnight bells chimed.

Chapter XI

MOVING TO THE FRONT — HOW TOM HYDE AND DAN CHUTE DIED

W HEN orders to leave for the front came from the General-issimo on the morning of the 16th February, 1937, there was an outburst of most cheerful enthusiasm, followed by the singing of the "Soldier's Song," our national anthem.

There were many in the bandera who had received their baptism of fire in the fight for Irish freedom, but the majority were about to go under fire for the first time, and what their reaction might be was naturally the cause of grave concern to me. They had received a long course of training, however, under skilled instructors, and were considered thoroughly efficient, and well prepared to go into action.

We were to leave at noon next day, and there was little sleep in the remaining hours.

Solemn High Mass was celebrated next morning in the church of San Domingo, and afterwards the Bishop, who had presided, came to the barracks where, walking along the ranks, he blessed each man. His Lordship blessed, too, the ambulance which had been sent to us by the Irish Christian Front.

Every house in Cáceres was decorated with flags and bunting in honour of the bandera, and thousands of people assembled at the railway station and along the streets.

Under normal conditions the journey would take about five hours, but it was five o'clock next day before Torrijos was reached, having been twenty-six hours on the way.

The first interruption of the journey was, in truth, a startling one. At the station next from Cáceres the driver of the train was taken off by the officer in charge of the local Nationalist troops, interrogated and searched.

In his possession, I was informed, documents were found which proved beyond doubt that he was in conspiracy with the enemy for the destruction of the train. It was intended, apparently, that at a certain point he should release his controls, jump to safety himself, and leave the heavily-laden train to hurtle down a steep decline, with the virtual certainty that it would leave the track and dash over a precipice.

We had good reason to be grateful for the efficiency of General Franco's intelligence service in averting an inglorious disaster at the outlet.

There was some delay at this station before another driver was secured, the enemy agent having been handed over for trial by the military courts.

A second narrow escape occurred when the train rumbled through Plasencia Junction just a few minutes before the place was bombed from the air.

At Navalmoral there was a long delay because of the damage to the line. The town had been bombed and over thirty children killed when leaving school the previous day.

On arrival in Torrijos the local commandant delivered instruction from General Orgaz, who was in charge of the division, that the bandera was to proceed at once by train to Terrejón, and from there to march by road the seven miles to Valdemora.

At dark we were in Terrejón, a wrecked village, its streets torn by shells, and littered with wrecked cars and fallen masonry. We had considerable difficulty here in securing a guide, for not a soul was to be seen. The Spanish officers accompanying us were strangers to the locality, and a mistake might be serious, as we were within a few miles of the front line. A small boy appeared at last as if from nowhere, and agreed to come with us to Valdemora.

The long train journey had been a severe trial, but the men shouldered their kits uncomplaining, set out in the darkness, cold and hungry, on the two hours' march, and Valdemora was reached at midnight.

For the first time since leaving Ireland the food problem threatened to be serious. Hitherto Captain Finnerty, the Irish Quartermaster, had charge of the commissariat and the quantity and quality left nothing to be desired. On the bandera leaving Cáceres, however, the Spanish authorities had accepted responsibility. The last meal (with the exception of a cup of coffee at Talavera that morning at nine) was in Cáceres the previous morning. At Valdemora the men certainly anticipated a hot meal, but after a wait of about two hours they were issued a mug of coffee and a tin of bully beef each. At this time anything in the way of food was welcome and every tin was emptied. After this experience our own Quartermaster again resumed responsibility.

When I reached Valdemora I found instructions awaiting me to have the bandera on parade at 6 a.m., preparatory to advancing later to occupy the front line trenches beyond the town of Ciempozuelos on the Jarama front. General Franco, to whom I was directly responsible, had told me that the bandera would be given second or third line positions before moving to the front line trenches. I did not seek or desire this privilege, and when the order came that we should proceed direct to the front line I accepted it cheerfully as did every man in the bandera. I felt, however, that after the hardships endured by the officers and men during the two previous days, the order to parade at dawn was unreasonable. I set out at once to see General Orgaz at Navalcarnero—forty miles away, and obtained his agreement to having the dawn parade called off. At 4 a.m. I was back at Valdemora and informed Major Dalton that the parade was off, but that marching orders for Ciempozuelos at 11 a.m. stood.

Accordingly the men slept for a few hours. Most of them lay that winter's night on tiled floors in a wrecked convent of which the walls and staircases were bespattered with the blood of the nuns who had been murdered there a week before. Some slept in lorries, others by the wayside, and all were disturbed by the unaccustomed thunder of artillery.

I left for Toledo at 5 a.m. to report the arrival of the bandera to the Military Governor there, and to make arrangements for transport and communications. Returning to Valdemora at 11 a.m. I found that the bandera had already moved off towards Ciempozuelos. I followed.

About a mile from the town I learned that there had been an engagement in which Lieutenant Tom Hyde, Lieutenant Bove, Sergeant Calvo and Legionary Dan Chute had been killed.

Immediately the bandera set out the sound of heavy artillery fire could be heard only a short distance away, and soon the curling puffs of smoke indicated where the shells were falling. Clearly the guns were directed on the main road, which was in uninterrupted view of the enemy. The bandera in extended order formation, therefore, took a bye-road on the advice of the senior Spanish officer present, Captain Botana.

When about a mile from Ciempozuelos a body of troops was observed advancing towards the Irish bandera, and in its line of route. The Irish bandera halted, and after consultation Lieutenant Bove, the Spanish officer attached to "A," the leading company, declared that the other troops were friendly. Captain O'Sullivan, accompanied by Lieutenant Bove, Sergeant-Major Timlin, Sergeant Calvo (Spanish interpreter) and Legionary McMahon thereupon went forward to meet the oncoming troops, the Irish bandera remaining halted at a distance from the others of about four hundred yards.

The other troops held their rifles at the ready. Eight paces from them Lieutenant Bove saluted the officer in charge and, addressing him in Spanish, said: "*Bandera Irlandese del Tercio.*"

Instantly, the captain to whom he spoke stepped back one pace, drew his revolver, and fired point blank at Lieutenant

Bove, but missed him. Captain O'Sullivan and Lieutenant Bove quickly returned the fire from their revolvers. "The enemy," shouted Lieutenant Bove, and then turned to double back with the others to his company—under a heavy fusillade. Lieutenant Bove and Sergeant Calvo were killed before they had retreated more than ten yards. Captain O'Sullivan, Sergeant Timlin and Legionary McMahon got back safely. Their escape was not short of miraculous.

"Open fire," ordered Captain O'Sullivan. A rapid exchange of machine-gun and rifle fire continued for about five minutes. Then the aggressors retreated, leaving more than half their number dead on the field.

Lieutenant Tom Hyde, of Cork, who was leading No. 1 section of "A" company, fell mortally wounded from a burst of machine-gun fire in the neck, which severed the carotid artery. This was our first casualty, and was followed immediately by that of Dan Chute, of Kerry, whose death was also instantaneous. John Hoey of Dublin was seriously wounded and spent several months in hospital.

The Irish bandera went on its way to Ciempozuelos under continued heavy gun-fire.

At Ciempozuelos we learned that the troops responsible for the attack on our bandera were a bandera of General Franco's army from the Canary Islands.

An inquiry was at once held, and complete responsibility for the encounter was placed on the leader of the Canary Island bandera, who had fired on Lieutenant Bove. The Irish bandera was held blameless, and highly complimented for coolness, steadiness and determination.

The officer in charge of the islanders had been killed in the encounter, with his second in command. The surviving officers were courtmartialled and the bandera disbanded.

There is a standing regulation in the Spanish army that when a body of troops "A" is to meet a body of friendly troops "B" marching in the opposite direction, the officer commanding the sector is to arrange for an officer from "A" to march at the head of "B" and *vice versa*. This regulation, which was specially necessary in our case, as we were foreigners, had unfortunately not been enforced, and hence the calamity.

I resolved in consequence to take advantage of my privilege of direct approach to General Franco while the bandera remained in this sector.

The Generalissimo, whom I saw two days afterwards, expressed his deep sympathy on our losses, and his high appreciation of the courageous conduct of the Irish troops in their first engagement.

Of Tom Hyde I can say that of all the men in the bandera he was best prepared for death. He led an exemplary life, he was a shining example to his fellow officers, and was easily the most popular man in the Brigade. He had won a first-class record in the struggle for Irish independence. He was one of my most trusted and loyal comrades and the finest character I ever knew. He died bravely as he would have wished, leading his countrymen to the front line of the fight for the faith.

Dan Chute of Tralee died bravely. He was a God-fearing, self-respecting member of the Brigade and was beloved by his comrades. He was one of the first to volunteer for service in Spain, and travelled with the first Kerry contingent. His widowed mother, when she received from me the message that meant she had lost her only son, said simply: "Although there's a load on my heart, I offer my boy to God, for Whom he fought."

Lieutenant Bove was most popular with all his Spanish and Irish comrades; officers and men alike. When the first party of the Irish Brigade reached Spain he came to me and asked to be attached to us. I at once accepted him, and I had named him as adjutant and aide-de-camp to the Irish commander if a second bandera should arrive.

Sergeant Calvo, a fine fellow, had also offered his services at the outset as an interpreter. He had given invaluable aid in the bandera's training, and died while discharging his duties.

The bodies were taken to an improvised hospital at Valdemora, embalmed, and a guard of honour placed. I returned to Cáceres to arrange for a military funeral, and at the request of the Mayor the remains were brought back, over two hundred miles, for burial in special vaults there.

At the High Mass for the Brigade on the morning we left for the front Tom Hyde bore the Irish tri-colour in the sanctuary. At the Requiem High Mass for the repose of his soul in the same church only four days afterwards the same flag draped his bier.

After Mass the four coffins, on which the Mayor placed the Irish and Spanish flags, were placed on gun carriages covered with beautiful wreaths. The funeral was the largest ever seen in Cáceres, the Bishop walked immediately behind the gun carriage accompanied by the Military Governor, the Mayor, the chiefs of the army and police, and followed by a battalion of troops, a battalion of the Felange, a battalion of the Requetes, a company of Civil Guards, a huge concourse of little boys and girls in uniform, each unit headed by its band.

The priests of the diocese in their surplices walked in front of the gun carriages, led by the Vicar-General carrying the Cross. In the cemetery the Military Governor delivered a touching oration, the artillery on an adjacent hill fired a salute of guns, the buglers sounded the last post, after which the Bishop pronounced the final absolution.

Cáceres, which had been bedecked in a lively farewell to the Brigade only a few days before, mourned now for our loss. Windows were shuttered, flags flew at half-mast, and almost the entire population: men, women and children, walked in the cortege, or stood as the funeral passed, in silent sympathy.

At home in Ireland there was universal sympathy. Many County Councils and other public bodies and organisations passed resolutions of condolence, and the churches were crowded at the Requiem Masses celebrated in Dublin, Midleton and Tralee, for those who had fallen first in battle for our high cause.

Chapter XII

CIEMPOZUELOS

C IEMPOZUELOS was a town of the dead when we arrived. Apart from Moorish troops, who left next day, and half a dozen Civil Guards, there was not a living person to be seen in streets or houses.

Only a few days before our occupation the town had been taken by Franco's troops in one of the bloodiest battles of the war. When the Reds were driven out they left over a thousand dead, many still unburied or only half-buried with a few inches of clay. One of our first duties was to dispose as best we could of the decomposing bodies which were to be seen everywhere; in the gardens and yards, in the river which runs through the town, and in the olive grove through which our main line of trenches ran. Ciempozuelos had been an important Red centre, and they left after them in their offices, which evidently had been evacuated rather suddenly, many files and records containing valuable information.

Sergeant-Major (later Lieutenant) Timlin thus describes the bandera's entry:

"The day was well advanced when 'A' company entered the town under cover of shell-racked buildings, finding desolation on all sides. The atmosphere seemed to be charged with an eerie expectancy. Conversations were carried on in whispers, as if the sound of a voice might disturb something unknown and unseen. Anxious glances were cast from side to side, endeavouring to pierce the depths of walls and barriers and learn the cause of this deathly stillness. And still the men marched on through the town and alongside the wide plaza.

"Suddenly the air was rent with a terrific explosion, made greater by the previous quiet, and followed by another, and still another. Shells were coming screeching through the air, ploughing up the roads and knocking the sides and tops from already partly demolished buildings.

"A halt was called in sight of a railway station, where we first caught sight of humans apart from ourselves. These were Moors arrayed in long multi-coloured robes and holding rifles cradled in their arms. They were tall and dark-skinned, adorned with beards and moustaches; turbans enveloped the tops of their heads. They observed the single approach of our Spanish liaison officer, Lieutenant Silva, with a tranquil awareness. With Sergeant Gabe Lee (later killed in action), I entered several houses on a tour of inspection. It required no great stretch of imagination to visualise the haste and terror in which some of these houses were vacated. Children's toys were trampled on, babies' shawls and bottles strewn about—one could almost hear the wailing of the mothers.

"Lieutenant Silva returned after an interval and informed me that we had arrived at our new position, which we were to occupy immediately. The station building was the guardhouse and soon a machine-gun post was taken over from the Moors. In front of the station were a plateau and twin hills separating the Reds from our position. There were machine-gun and observation posts on the top of the hills, and we took these over also from the departing Moors."

Ciempozuelos is situated fifteen miles from Madrid, on the railway line, and near the main road leading to Cordova and Málaga. The bandera was responsible for holding the front line along the Jarama River from Aranjuez on the south to San Martin de la Vega on the north, a length of over eight miles, with Titulcia—a strongly fortified enemy post—across the river, immediately opposite our central position, and Chinchon, enemy divisional headquarters a few miles farther back in the mountains.

The position we held was one of the most vulnerable on the Jarama River, and was under shell fire daily, sometimes for hours at a stretch. On one recorded occasion no fewer than fifty-eight shells fell in twenty-two minutes. About one in every three of the shells which came over, however, was "dud", and the result was that our troops had little respect for them. By this I do not wish to convey that our men took unnecessary risks or were in any sense reckless. If such had been the case we would have had many more Irish graves in Spain.

There were many astonishing escapes. A corporal of a trench mortar section was completely buried in clay, but was nothing the worse when dug out by his comrades. A shell cut the blanket of an officer as he was resting in his dugout, but left him unscathed. Nevertheless the spirit and morale of all ranks remained splendid.

Our advance outposts were assailed frequently from an armoured train manned by members of the International brigade, whose pronouncedly Cockney voices could be heard clearly from our lines.

The railway line to Madrid was intact to within about seven hundred yards of Ciempozuelos railway station, and the armoured train was able to make its incursions in the shelter of the surrounding hills.

There was also sniping of our positions, and of course our troops returned the fire vigorously, but with what effect we do not know. We had several wounded in these engagements, the most serious case being that of Tom McMullen, who had his left leg amputated. This young man, an athlete well known in Co. Mayo, showed remarkable courage when it was conveyed to him in Grianon hospital that to save his life it would be necessary to amputate the leg. Doctors and nurses told me that he was the bravest soldier that ever entered the hospital, as he certainly was the most popular.

Apart from gun-fire, officers and men in the trenches endured much hardship during February and March. The trenches were shallow and badly constructed, affording little or no protection from wind or rain. The bandera set about making improvements, straightening out lines, establishing more advanced posts, constructing gun emplacements, and so on, but owing to the length of the line we held, the order for transfer to another front was received before the job was completed.

The rain was torrential, and the trenches, being on the crest of a hill, were exposed to the storm; often they were flooded. The boots supplied were not waterproof, the little forage cap was useless for keeping the head anyway warm, and there was no such thing as a waterproof ground-sheet. The Moors, who had occupied the trenches immediately before the Irish bandera, had collected quite a quantity of mattresses from the wreckage down town. These would have been very useful for the dugouts, but had to be discarded except for outside shelters, as they were alive with lice. The lice, indeed, caused our troops more annoyance than the shells of the enemy. A well-known powder was sent from Ireland, but the pests of the Jarama dugouts seemed to thrive on it.

Wet clothing caused serious trouble. For twelve weeks the men had no change of outside or inside clothing. There was no grumbling. Men who were hardly able to stand on their feet would not report sick. The continual wettings had their effect later however in our hospital cases of rheumatism, pleurisy, serious coughs and colds. Early in March Major Dalton fell ill. He was sent to the Central Military hospital in Cáceres for treatment, but later was reluctantly compelled to return to Ireland. He was an experienced, tactful and popular officer, all ranks had the utmost confidence in him, and his departure from amongst us caused very sincere regret.

Captain O'Sullivan took over charge from Major Dalton, with Captain Quinn as second in command. Captain Quinn was one of our outstanding officers. I consulted him on every problem that arose and his judgment was always sound. No officer gave more personal attention to his men. When I visited his dugout, often in the middle of the night, I invariably found that he was doing a round of the trenches. I could never understand how he was able to keep on his feet, with so little rest or sleep.

Captain Skeffington-Smyth and Lieutenant Nangle preceded the Irish brigade to Spain, and had early distinguished themselves in the legion. I met them in Salamanca, where they offered their services and I commissioned them as our advance liaison officers. Captain Smyth served as an officer in the Irish Guards. In Spain he assumed the name of Michael Fitzpatrick. Lieutenant Gilbert Nangle served for a time in the French Foreign Legion.

Over one hundred young Spaniards who had just completed their training as cadets were attracted by the Irish brigade and offered to join. About twenty of these were attached in various capacities and rendered useful service. Practically all were sons of grandees and had titles. Spaniards of Irish descent offered to form a special section of the brigade. Many English, French and Portuguese reported to me for duty, the Irish in the U.S.A. offered to send a cavalry regiment, and I had applications from Palestine, Egypt, and several European countries. It was considered advisable however to maintain the brigade as a distinct Irish unit.

The bandera's duty was very severe. Each company spent four days in the trenches, then two in the town, resting. The resting company had to find guards and pickets, also to provide a section each day as a protective party for a German engineering corps some miles away. The German commanding officer, Colonel Von Thomas, had paid us the compliment of requesting Irish infantry protection. Most of the Germans spoke English and soon there were close friendships between the Irish and German ranks. The German officers, too, were always very eager to co-operate with us; I had many conferences with the Colonel and his staff.

I should here express my gratitude to the Military Governor of Toledo for his invariable kindness and hospitality to myself personally, and for supplying transport to bring us food supplies, though the bandera was outside his command.

Soon after we had occupied Ciempozuelos some of the townsfolk who had escaped the Red savageries began to return in one's and two's. They had lost all that was dear to them and returned to the spot where they were born, hoping against hope that some of their missing loved ones might also return. They had heartbreaking stories to tell of the days of terror in the town, and of the horrible ways in which their husbands and sons had been butchered, or compelled to join the Red forces; of the fate of wives and daughters they did not care to speak. So far as they could, our troops helped these pathetic refugees to re-inhabit their shattered homes.

One of our company headquarters was formerly the residence of the most eminent surgeon in the province. The doctor, in the presence of his family, was put on his own operating table, I was told, and with his own surgical instruments his nails were pulled off, he was made write his name on the walls in his own blood, and his eyes were removed before he died. A surviving daughter visited what was once her comfortable home, while the Irish bandera was in occupation, and told us her tragic story.

The only building in the town which had escaped was the mental hospital for women, one of the largest in Spain and filled to overflowing. There were over one thousand inmates, mostly young women and girls, of whom many had entered because of their experiences during the Red occupation of the district. That even this building, which had been the Red headquarters, had escaped was attributable to the fact that many of the unhappy inmates were related to Red officers and men, who had lived in the province. The immunity of the place continued while we were in the town, and it was considered extraordinary that while hundreds of shells struck other buildings, not one touched the institution.

The nuns who were in charge of the hospital showed a devotion to their duties which was wonderful. Notwithstanding the din of cannon, night and day, and the screams of the unfortunate lunatics as one explosion followed another, the sisters went about their work as calmly as if conditions were entirely normal. They had terrible trials during the occupation of the institution by the Reds. Many had been killed, some had endured what was worse than death to them, and some had been carried off by the retreating forces.

The four churches and the convents in the town were no more than shells. The altars, pulpits, etc., had been smashed to fragments and the hammer and sickle had been painted on the walls. Many of the Irish volunteers found burned pieces of sacred vestments which they carefully collected from the debris and sent home to their friends in Ireland as silent witnesses to the reality of the Red terror. In the cellars of the ruined convents the bodies of nuns were discovered.

We were told that the first Mass in Ciempozuelos for over six months was that celebrated by our chaplain on the day after the bandera arrived.

THE THIRTEENTH

O N 13TH MARCH, 1937, our Irish bandera went "over the top".

I had gone to Cáceres on 12th March to receive reports as to progress made in the arrangements for another bandera from Ireland, and late in the evening received the news that our men were to take part early next morning in an advance on Titulcia, the town to which I have referred. At once I set out on the two-hundred-mile journey and reached Ciempozuelos about midnight. Two-thirds of the bandera were still on duty in the trenches and the remainder were resting.

I held a conference with all available officers, Irish and Spanish, and discussed plans for the difficult part allotted to us in the advance—a feint direct movement on the town to deceive the enemy and divide his forces, while two other banderas were advancing on it from the north.

At 5 a.m. our trenches had been temporarily occupied by a Spanish bandera, and our troops in full war kit were ready to move off from the plaza of Ciempozuelos. Tired of the inactivity of the trenches, and full of hope to get into closer touch with the enemy, the volunteers marched off with a serene determination on every face. Shells screeched overhead as our batteries were answered by the enemy's guns.

A squadron of Moorish cavalry had gone ahead. Immediately it reached the open plain intensive artillery fire had been opened on it. The squadron retreated almost at once to the base, leaving a few men and horses dead on the field. Undaunted, the Irish bandera moved steadily on in battle order, deploying across a wide plain, with only growing grass and an occasional clump of hay for cover.

From the outset the enemy artillery found correct range, and between 7 a.m. and 9 a.m. the commander of our supporting battery recorded that two hundred and fifty shells had fallen on the plain. Unlike the shells directed at our trenches and at the town during the previous four weeks, there were no "duds" now; every shell exploded.

The bandera advanced steadily. From my position I could observe our volunteers creep along while a veritable rain of shells exploded in their midst. The shells fell four at a time, and the smoke of one set had not subsided when the whistle of the next was heard. Now, a soldier moved to take cover in a clump of hay, then, the hay was enveloped in smoke. About mid-day, when the troops had advanced about three miles from the town, no fewer than four hundred shells had been estimated to have fallen. Major H. F. Recke, a German officer who was with me, said that never before had he seen such accurate range-finding, or such a high percentage of shells exploding.

At noon we had a consultation in the artillery officers' observation post. The officer commanding the sector was present, also the divisional artillery officer, and General Franco's representative with the bandera, Captain Camino. These experienced officers estimated that we had between two and three hundred killed out of our seven hundred odd, and the advisability of advancing further with our number so depleted was considered.

Our stretcher-bearers were busy at this stage and the ambulances were rushing to and from a ruin which served as a dressing-station. The dressing-station too was being shelled periodically, but without effect.

I decided to leave the observation post and see the position for myself. Shortly after I had left it, a shell fell beside the observation post, though no damage was done. Another post was hurriedly occupied, and about five minutes afterwards a shell fell on the post previously used and demolished it.

Accompanied by the Duke of Algeciras, also Captain Gunning, Father Mulrean and Corporal Tony Monaghan, I made my way right down to the plain. I was surprised and delighted to find that up to then there had been no fatal casualties whatever and only a few wounded.

The advance continued, the shells still falling, but officers, N.C.O.'s and men, were all in high spirits.

In the afternoon the armoured train manned by the English Reds made an appearance. Hitherto, while our troops were in the trenches, it had been ineffective. Now, from its position on the slope of the hill, it commanded the plain where our troops were alternately advancing and taking the little cover available. Immediately a set of shell burst, the guns of the train came into action, as it was thought the bursting shells would cause our troops to raise their heads and reveal their positions—but there was not a move. Trench mortar fire from the train, however, is believed to have killed John McSweeney of Tralee.

At my request a party of Spanish engineering officers had a few nights previously placed a mine under the railway track at a point where the train was accustomed to halt. On the thirteenth it halted at exactly the same spot.

Hopefully I watched the engineer press the electric appliance; but it failed to explode the mine.

Another attempt was made some time afterwards, and there was a shattering explosion in which railway sleepers and earth went skywards. Again the train escaped; apparently a few minutes before the explosion it had moved back about a hundred yards to get a better view of the plain below. Whether the train was damaged is not known as it was hidden by the hills from view of the engineers' dugout.

At nightfall the head of the bandera had reached the Jarama River. Orders were issued to return to Ciempozuelos.

The rain was coming down in torrents, every man was soaked to the skin, the plain had to be searched for dead or wounded. It took nearly three hours after that very strenuous day for the return journey in full kit with machine-guns and stretchers, and helping those along who from sheer exhaustion were unable to walk.

I should here compliment our Red Cross section, especially Legionaires Bergin of Tipperary, Roche of Cork, Brophy of Dublin, and McCloskey of Louth, the ambulance driver, for their conspicuous bravery on the field, in attending to wounded comrades and carrying them to safety under heavy shell-fire. They brought back three of our men fatally injured: Sergeant-Major Gabe Lee of Dublin and Legionaires Bernard Horan and Tom Foley of Kerry. Though rushed to Grianon hospital by ambulance and given the best attention possible, they died within a few days.

The following were also brought in suffering from shrapnel wounds: Mick O'Connor of Dublin, whose life was almost despaired of for several weeks, Sergeant Lawlor of Carlow, Corporal Donnelly of Louth, Legionaires P. Gilbert of Limerick, Tom McGrath of Cork, and Mark Price of Dublin. They were sent to Grianon hospital that evening, and later transferred to other hospitals further from the firing line.

It was only by the mercy of God and the skill and judgment shown by our comparatively inexperienced officers that the Irish bandera was not annihilated on that fateful 13th March. Rifles were split in two in their hands, packs were cut into pieces on their backs, they were time and again covered with showers of earth and stones as shell after shell exploded.

The Reds believed that the bandera had in fact been annihilated. In a broadcast from Madrid on the same night it was announced that the Irish had been "completely wiped out" in an engagement during the day. That this falsehood was generally accepted was clear from the comment of the leader of a party of Red soldiers who deserted their lines early in the following week, and came across to us to surrender their arms. Lieutenant Nangle, who spoke Spanish fluently, received them. He announced that he was an officer of the 15th (Irish) bandera.

Said the leader of the Red party: "Oh, no, señor, you cannot be. The Irish bandera was put out of existence last Saturday. Not a man survived. There was no life left on the plain."

They were astonished to see our troops fresh and well, and could not understand how our casualties had been so few.

The operation was disappointing to the Irish bandera. They had anticipated getting into close contact with the enemy, and instead had been obliged to endure eleven hours continuous shelling from enemy batteries miles away. They saw their comrades wounded beside them, and had not an opportunity of firing a shot in retaliation.

This, of course, is one of the greatest trials in modern warfare, and was particularly severe on our keen, enthusiastic Irish volunteers.

Had they succeeded in meeting the enemy infantry I have no doubt they would have given as effective an account of themselves as they did when attacked on their way to Ciempozuelos, a month before.

The only support we had from other branches of the service was one battery of artillery sending shells at an invisible enemy behind the mountains, and in the afternoon, a short visit from a fleet of planes.

The concentration of enemy gunfire on us, as we afterwards learned, was due to the fact that the other banderas on whose account we were to make the feint direct movement on Titulcia, had not got away from their base.

On return to Ciempozuelos from the plain, the bandera was given a hot meal, the preparation of which, for nearly seven hundred men, was a big job, considering the limited facilities in the wrecked houses which served as kitchens; and while they ate the rain came flooding through the improvised roofs. The meal

over, they had to re-occupy the trenches, the bandera in tempo-
rary occupation having been ordered elsewhere. Without any
change of clothing—they had, as I have indicated, no change
available—the volunteers set off sturdily in the rainstorm to
spend the night in the water-logged trenches.

I saw them as they moved off and there was not a murmur
of complaint. If the Irish people could only realise what these
brave men and boys endured so cheerfully, in the cause of Christianity, I think more appreciation would be shown of their sacrifice.

They could not get a stimulant. I would have been very
happy, indeed, to offer each man a "tot of brandy" that night.
We have heard of drunkenness in the Brigade. I did not see it,
but if an Irish soldier did take too much drink (and it would not
take much alcohol to upset men under the conditions I have
outlined above), I could appreciate the reason.

With the secrecy which it was obviously necessary to
observe, it was not possible to investigate each applicant's past
conduct, and a few doubtful characters managed to get away in
the rush. It is neither just nor charitable, however, to attempt to
injure the fair name of the Brigade because of the few, nor to
make it more difficult to find employment for its decent, self-
respecting members, who numbered ninety-eight per cent of the
total.

When the trenches had been re-occupied still another bandera arrived to take over. Our men came back to the town, and
went to rest in clothes and blankets saturated with rain. And
their rest was not to last long.

I was early astir myself, owing to my anxiety for troops
undergoing such hardships, and reached our headquarters at
6 a.m. There I was informed that an order had just been received
over the private wire from divisional headquarters that the bandera was to advance again at 8 a.m. that morning, to take the
town of Titulcia. This order involved:

1. The advance through the same plain on which the enemy
had continuously rained shells the previous day, finding perfect

range, and with practically no cover. I estimated that before we could reach the bridge leading to the town we should lose at least half the bandera.

2. We were an open target for enemy air bombs.

3. The bridge, which was our only line of approach to the town, was probably mined. The enemy would likely explode the mine when half our men were across—thus dividing our forces.

4. The enemy was strongly entrenched with machine-guns trained on the bridge we had to cross.

5. We had neither tank nor aircraft support.

6. Assuming that a remnant of the bandera reached the town we would find ourselves completely isolated, being the only troops east of the river for miles on either side.

7. There was no previous reconnaissance, and none of the Spanish officers attached to bandera had a knowledge of the area or of the dispositions, strength, or equipment of the enemy in possession.

I had a consultation with the Spanish staff of the sector, the artillery officers, and the Irish officers. All were of the opinion that there was no chance whatever of the success of the operation, and that in the attempt to carry it out there would be a huge loss of life. On the one hand I was confronted with the almost certain probability of the sacrifice of the entire Brigade in an operation which I believed, after hearing the views of the officers on the spot, had not even one per cent, chance of success; and on the other hand, with a definite order from divisional headquarters.

A decision had to be taken, and at once. I ordered a full parade of the bandera, with instructions that it be held in readiness to advance. Having ordered the stand-to, I set out myself to see General Saliquet at field general headquarters at Gosque, about fifteen miles away. The General saw me when I arrived. Well I realised how serious it was for a subordinate to question an order from a superior. Having informed him of the position, I said that as leader of the Irish Brigade I had taken upon myself, whatever the consequence might be, the grave responsibility of ordering the troops to remain at their base pending further instructions.

General Saliquet appeared very much surprised, and I at once formed the opinion that he was not hitherto aware of the order. He authorised me in any event, to have the operation called off.

A few days later General Franco and General Mola visited the scene of operations at Ciempozuelos. I was in Cáceres attending the funerals of our killed at the time, but a message was sent to me to meet the Generalissimo early next morning at Navalcarnero, a few miles from Madrid. There we discussed the position and General Franco expressed the view that Titulcia could not be taken by direct attack from Ciempozuelos unless supported by strong flank attacks, and that several banderas working in co-operation would be necessary. He also confirmed my belief that the bridge was mined and that the town was a fortress.

I felt very happy after this interview, inasmuch as while I had succeeded in saving the lives of those who had shown so much loyalty and trust in my leadership, I had at the same time now received a renewal of the confidence of the Generalissimo to whom I was directly responsible. I shall probably never know who was responsible for the order, which under ordinary circumstances would have been so welcome, but which might well have had such disastrous consequences. At the time of writing Titulcia has not fallen.

Gabriel Lee, who died of wounds received on the 13th, held the responsible rank of Sergeant-Major, and was one of the finest soldiers in the Brigade, fearless and popular. He joined the Irish Volunteers in his early teens, and later served in the National Army, where he reached the rank of Commandant. He received very severe wounds from the shrapnel of a shell which burst beside him, cutting his rifle in two. I was present when he was brought in on a stretcher. He was suffering intense pain, still he tried to smile when he recognised me, and asked me to take charge of his little personal property. He improved somewhat in hospital for the first day or two, but it was obvious from the beginning that only death could bring relief. His last words to me before he died were: "I wish to die in my Irish green shirt, in respect to my leader."

John McSweeney, Tom Foley and Bernard Horan, all of Tralee, were close companions and had travelled together from Galway to Spain. They did honour to their country in giving their lives for her Faith on a foreign field. Please God Ireland will honour their memory some day.

Chapter XIV

HONOUR TO OUR DEAD

A T CÁCERES our dead were buried, and there too most of our wounded and sick were tended in hospitals.

It was at the Mayor's request that the bodies of those killed on the 13th at Ciempozuelos were brought back there to be interred in four special vaults side by side with those of Tom Hyde and Dan Chute, in a place of honour in the city's new mausoleum. The Bishop of Cáceres presided at the Requiem Masses, which were attended by the military and civil authorities. A State funeral was given, and the tribute of the people of Cáceres was even more impressive than before. Massed military bands played the march of the legion before the vaults, and St. Mary's Pipe Band, from Dublin, made its first appearance in Spain, at the funeral, playing the lament "Flowers of the Forest."

Our troops on the occasion of church parades and ceremonial functions were under a disadvantage in marching to Spanish music with Spanish bands, and in the beginning these were unable to play our national anthem. When leaving for Ireland I had been requested to make an effort to bring an Irish pipers' band to Spain. In Dublin the St. Mary's Pipe Band very generously volunteered their free services, fully equipped with new pipes, drums and costumes. It created a splendid impression everywhere in Spain and enhanced the prestige of the brigade.

It was invited to the various hospitals, and given pride of place in military ceremonials, and at social functions.

Captain Patrick Hughes of Dublin, who travelled to Spain with St. Mary's Band, had charge of the Irish troops at the depot and in the hospitals in Cáceres.

It was not until the worst of the winter was over that the terrible hardships in the trenches began to affect our troops. The weather at La Maranosa, to which they were transferred, was much milder than at Ciempozuelos, there was very little rain, though the nights remained bitterly cold. The conditions at Ciempozuelos were bound however to have their effect. For the first time, large numbers reported on the sick parade each morning. Before long, no fewer than one hundred and fifty were removed to hospital, and four of our crusaders succumbed. Legionary John Walsh, of Midleton, Co. Cork, died while the brigade was still at the front, and Sergeant Tom Troy, of Clare, died on the eve of our departure from Spain. They, too, were given military funerals and buried at Cáceres in vaults side by side with their fallen Irish comrades. Eunan McDermott of Ballyshannon, Co. Donegal, and Thomas Doyle of Roscrea, Co. Tipperary, were treated at general medical headquarters, Salamanca. The doctors and also Father McCabe, Rector, and Father O'Hara, Vice-Rector of the Irish College there, were unremitting in care of them, but from the beginning little hopes were entertained for their recovery. They died after a rather prolonged illness, and were buried with military honours in special vaults in the Salamanca City Cemetery.

Since the Brigade returned to Ireland, the following volunteers have died at home as a result of the Spanish campaign:

John McGrath of Galway.
Mat Barlow of Longford.
Jack Cross of Limerick.
P. Dwyer of Clonmel.

Michael Weymes of Dublin, who elected to remain in Spain, was killed in action near Madrid. He was son of P. J. Weymes, former M.P. and Chairman of Westmeath County Council. Michael served in the Fianna, National Army and Civic Guard. He was a brave and fearless soldier and very popular.

Special praise is due to the medical and nursing staffs of Grianon and Ciempozuelos hospitals for their attention and kindness to our wounded; also to the doctors in Torrijos hospital, who supplied medical requisites, but above all to Colonel O'Choa, the chief of medical service in the city and province of Cáceres, who at one time had over a hundred Irish patients in his charge. He gave a very large proportion of his time to them, and many Irish volunteers owe their lives to his skilful attention.

The response to our call for Irish medical officers was very disappointing, I may say; our wounded and sick in hospitals were all the time under the care of Spanish doctors, none of whom could offer advice or comfort to our men in English.

Dr. Conor Martin of Dublin, very kindly looked after our interests in regard to medical supplies. The consignment which did reach us was invaluable, and showed that Dr. Martin had full knowledge of what would be useful.

Colonel McCabe, M.B., Hon. Director of Medical Services for the brigade, also placed at our disposal his wide experience of war medical requirements, and wrote some useful memoranda on the more common trench diseases and ailments, and on the preservation of the health of men on active service.

Towards the end of February too, Nurse MacGorisk and Nurse Mulvaney arrived from Ireland, and took up duty in the Central Military Hospital in Cáceres, where the majority of our sick were treated. They gave their services voluntarily, and rendered most excellent assistance. Untiring in their attention, day and night, they were soon recognised by the Spanish doctors as highly skilled in their noble profession. Miss O'Donnell, who is of Irish descent, and had been living with a family in the north of Spain for many years, also came to Cáceres to assist us.

Though not a qualified nurse, she gave splendid help as an interpreter between the Spanish doctors and the Irish patients.

About this time also Rev. Father O'Daly, of Enniskillen, who had been appointed chaplain to the second bandera, arrived. Unfortunately the second bandera did not reach Spain, but Father O'Daly, who received no remuneration whatsoever, remained with us. Moving quietly around in his own unostentatious way he soon became very popular with all ranks.

Our headquarters depot was still at Cáceres. All letters and cablegrams to and from our troops were sent there for censorship and dispatch, as General Franco had entrusted me with full responsibility in this respect. It was a big undertaking, as I had to read and censor as many as a thousand letters weekly, but the troops showed remarkable judgment, and rarely wrote anything which might be regarded as information of military importance, should the letters fall into the hands of the enemy.

Small batches of volunteers continued to arrive from Ireland and were sent to Cáceres for training. So confident were we of getting out at least another bandera that the Spanish training staff was kept intact to the end, and barrack accommodation retained.

Cáceres, indeed, has done honour in every way to the brigade, and through it, to Ireland. Though we hope in due course to bring home the bodies of our dead volunteers, they rest meantime in peace and homage.

Shortly before leaving Spain, I received the following letter from the Mayor of Cáceres:

"The Standing Committee of this Municipal Corporation, over which I have the honour to preside, wishing to render the merited homage of the greatest respect to the glorious dead of the Catholic Legion from Ireland, has agreed to the proposal of myself as President, to offer the vaults in which they have been interred in perpetuity, placing on the same slabs that will perpetuate the names of the heroes there at rest.

"On advising you of this decree, as leader of the Irish legion, I should like to indicate to you the veneration in which we shall here hold your fallen comrades, and to assure you that the city of Cáceres will know how to guard the memory of those who, while fighting for Spain, knew how to die gloriously for her.

"May God give you many years.

"Signed,

"LUCIANO LOPEZ HIDALGO,
"Mayor of Cáceres."

I sent the following reply:

"Your Excellency,—It is difficult for me to express adequately the emotion caused to me by the decree of the Municipal Corporation, offering perpetually the vaults where our comrades, who have fallen in defence of Spain and of the Catholic Faith, are interred, and also placing slabs on the vaults, by which means the Municipal Corporation of Cáceres so generously desires to perpetuate the names of our fallen in action.

"I appreciate in all its value the kind interest and the generosity which both yourself, as Mayor presiding, the Aldermen, as well as the whole citizens of Cáceres, have on so many occasions shown towards us. We have had outstanding proofs of the same on festive occasions, as well as on those sad and painful ones when we had to accompany the mortal remains of our fallen comrades to their last resting place.

"There is a desire in Ireland, which may perhaps be carried out, for the remains of the Irish volunteers, which now repose in the soil of this noble city, to be taken home to Ireland, their native land, once this war is over.

"In any case, I beg that you will accept, on my own behalf and on that of all the volunteers of the Irish Brigade, our deepest gratitude for such a noble and generous thought.

At the same time I would request you to transfer these sentiments to the Municipal Corporation, over which you so worthily preside, as well as to the people of Cáceres, who so nobly received us in their midst, and in whose city we have spent so many happy days.

"Permit me, in closing, to express to your Lordship my sentiments of the greatest respect and personal regard towards yourself."

The parents and other relatives of the fifteen Irish crusaders who gave their lives in the cause of Christianity bore their tribulations with splendid fortitude and resignation to God's holy will. In due course I believe the people of Ireland will show their appreciation of the sacrifice.

It was the mother of an Irish volunteer who honoured me by dedicating to me a poem of which I shall quote the concluding stanza:

> *Now take my blessing, son my dear,*
> *God keep you from all stain,*
> *And do not heed my poor weak tear,*
> *My loss is Ireland's gain;*
> *And if, returning not, one day*
> *For you they ask, I'll proudly say:*
> *'My son! he went to Spain.'*

LA MARANOSA — THE REQUETES

O N OCCUPYING Ciempozuelos the bandera had resolved to hold the section while an Irish soldier survived. We handed it over intact after five weeks occupation to a mixed brigade of Spaniards and Italians, nearly four times our strength numerically. The officer commanding, an Italian, when taking over from us, posted three men to our one and complained that he could not hold the line unless he got reinforcements.

The bandera had now hoped for a short rest, which was long overdue, in some town out of reach of the enemy shells. Instead it was sent to hold a section of a line on La Maranosa front, nine miles nearer to Madrid. The Spanish capital, which was only six miles away, was clearly visible from our lines, with the Hill of Angels on our left flank, and the València road on our right. The ruins of a factory served as bandera headquarters, and our kitchens were in the open, in little valleys between the hills.

Here the biggest problem was the water supply. Fresh water was not to be obtained nearer than eight miles. It was drawn by mules in cisterns across country, and usually had got warm, if not hot, before it reached us. The water in the Jarama River close by was condemned by the medical authorities, and the approach to it from our lines was in clear view of the enemy. Nevertheless, our lads frequently took a risk, and enjoyed a dip in its cooling waters. In the end, water was so scarce that it could only be had for cooking purposes, and was not available for washing or shaving. This was a great disadvantage, for our troops always desired to look clean and smart, and felt unhappy if they had not their accustomed morning shave. The Spaniards didn't seem to mind, and were quite content to shave once a fortnight or so, or to let their beards grow.

In Ciempozuelos, our bandera, except in the most advanced outposts, was out of range of rifle or machine-gun fire from the enemy, and the troops could move about in comparative safety. La Maranosa offered very little freedom of movement. The enemy had found accurate range of the only mountain path connecting our trenches and dugouts and accordingly it was only permitted to use this at night. If a man ventured to raise his head along it during the day, a trench mortar from the hill opposite banged the spot. Our troops had become accustomed to heavy artillery fire, and learned to avoid the shells. The silently-fired trench mortar was more dreaded, but—perhaps as a result—we had no casualties from it.

We had a number of men wounded, some seriously, in machine-gun and rifle exchanges. Not only the trenches, but the dugouts, where the troops rested, were on the crest of a range of hills without either cover or protection.

Major O'Sullivan, in a letter to his father, shows the risks which all the members of the bandera ran every day and every night in their dugouts at La Maranosa:

"General O'Duffy was away from us for a few days, as of course you can understand he has an amount of going about to do; but, nevertheless his one thought is for the boys, and to spend as much time as possible in the trenches with them. He returned here on Thursday night, and as usual, he occupied his dugout in the front line trenches.

"Thursday night was quiet except for an occasional burst of machine-gun fire, which by now does not cause us any loss of sleep, and yesterday morning the General seemed to enjoy his breakfast, a cup of coffee and bread, to the music

of bursting shells, which is an every-day and all-day programme. After breakfast Capt. Finnerty and I accompanied
him back to the brigade stores, in a disused and shell-
battered gas factory about a mile in the rear of our front line.

"Going there is always an ordeal, as there is no cover,
and the area is under shell-fire the whole day. You can
imagine our anxiety when the General is with us. As I have
often told you before, we would be in a very bad way in this
foreign land without his support and guidance, and, therefore, our anxiety on these occasions is shared by every individual member of the brigade.

"General O'Duffy spent from 9 a.m. until 9:30 p.m. in
Captain Finnerty's office, during which time he interviewed
every officer and N.C.O. and discussed at length the food,
clothing and water supply of the brigade—in fact, everything
that would add to the comfort and well-being of the men. I
might add that Captain Finnerty is a brick, and is doing won-
ders under trying conditions, as, of course, you can understand that food and the Spanish system of supplies are
entirely different from what we have been used to at home
in our 'wee' army.

"We returned about 10 p.m. to our private apartment in
the front line, and after a chat and smoking all the General's
'Sweet Aftons', which were a God-send, we retired from the
General's private suite. This is built with sandbags and
stones for side walls, and ground sheets for a roof, as are all
the other dugouts for officers and men. None of them is what
you would term bomb or shell-proof.

"We left the General to enjoy a well-earned rest, as we
thought, after a very hard day's work, at the same time hoping for a quiet night and a rest for ourselves; but, alas, our
hopes and dreams were shattered because at 3:30 a.m. we
were rudely awakened by the din of intense rifle-fire, coupled
with fierce trench-mortar and hand-grenade explosions.

"What was happening? Well, the boys were in action
again, repelling a determined night attack on our lines. To

add to my heavy responsibilities, you can picture my worry about the General's safety, because on this, as on all other occasions, he insisted on being with the boys, and sharing their dangers.

"Comparative quiet was restored about 5:30 a.m. and the reserves who had been rushed into the trenches were once more back in their dugouts to continue their interrupted sleep. The General, and the officers not on duty, also retired to get a few hours sleep before attending Mass, which is celebrated at 8:30 a.m. each morning in the front line by a Carlist chaplain.

"We were tucked in—of course, all we take off going to bed is our caps—when we were again compelled to turn out. This time our exit was, if anything, faster and more determined than the first, as the Reds opened up an intensive artillery barrage on our lines lasting for, roughly, two and a half hours.

"Captain Quinn and I made a bee-line for the General's dugout, which is next door to ours. At the entrance we bumped into Finnerty and Lieutenant Timlin, and to the accompaniment of a whistling shell, the four of us dived headlong in around the floor, burying the General in the dust. I can tell you he looked anything but a General when we had disentangled ourselves from the mess. The shell left a large gaping hole a few yards from the door.

"But this was only the start, as the Rocos (Reds) had not as yet found the accurate range. They pounded away, lobbing shells on both sides and in front of us, until at last, to our discomfort, and I might say to our expectations, they started to fall on the path immediately over the dugout.

"Two shells burst at the same time, not more than two yards above us and to the rear of the dugout. So great was the force of the explosion that Quinn and Timlin were hurled half-way out, and the General, Finnerty and myself were almost buried under a heap of falling sandbags and caved-in walls. This was certainly a lucky escape for us all, and particularly the General. It seemed to indicate that the prayers of the Irish people at home and abroad were at that moment answered, as the Reds lengthened their range and proceeded to shell the old gas factory. After dropping about twenty-five more shells they apparently retired for their morning coffee and rolls, leaving us in peace.

"Later we attended Mass. It is a glorious sight, and carries one back through the pages of Irish history, to our forefathers' fight for the Faith at home in the Penal Days. All available officers, N.C.O.'s and men, attend Mass every day, and large numbers are daily Communicants. I have often mentioned to you before the devotion to the sacraments of the members of the brigade, and I am sure you will be glad to learn that they are keeping up to the traditions of Catholic Ireland. Their outstanding devotion has been very favourably commented on by high dignitaries of the Church in Spain, all branches of the army, and the civilian population.

"The General is now leaving us for a few days, and when he is gone, we will breathe a sigh of relief, for we shall know he is safe."

After Mass I left the front for Cáceres. The shelling of the road or track from La Maranosa was intense. My car was hidden in smoke and dust from the bursting shells, and to add to the confusion I had a new driver—Captain Meade had gone on sick leave—who had no knowledge of the way out through the fields and sand dykes. I had more fear of the car overturning than I had of the falling shells, one of which actually fell at the back wheel of the car, but it was a dud and did no damage. I continued the journey.

At La Maranosa we had six batteries of artillery supporting us as against two at Ciempozuelos, and we had a number of anti-aircraft guns. All this, of course, contributed to closer enemy concentration on our lines, particularly of enemy planes, but these were kept at bay by our superior fighting planes. Our troops had a great thrill during one air attack.

Our anti-aircraft guns hit one of the Red planes as it came directly over our lines. It flew so low that one could almost talk to the pilot. As he passed over petrol was flowing from his machine and it was thought he would crash. Instead he glided through the foot-hills into the plains, out of sight of our guns, and to his own lines. Although he came to attack, one could not help admiring his coolness, and feeling glad that he escaped; death was certain had he come down among the rocks. He was undoubtedly a first-rate pilot.

What will ever remain in the hearts of the members of the Irish bandera as the happiest remembrance of La Maranosa was the association with two banderas of the Requetes, who held the section with us. The Requetes are the fighting arm of the Carlist movement, which put almost one hundred thousand men on the field. The Carlists, of course, are the followers of the Royal House of Don Carlos, and have never ceased to dispute the right of Alfonso to the throne of Spain. They are ardent Catholics, and where at all possible receive Holy Communion daily in the trenches. They are amongst the best soldiers in Franco's army, and are largely responsible for the successes of Irun, San Sebastián, Bilbao, Santander and Gijón. They not only held their own province of Navarra intact from the outset, but they drove the Red forces out of Northern Spain.

The Requetes, who wear traditional red berets, receive no pay, and their food and clothing are provided by the Carlist organisation. The late General Mola was one of themselves—he was their worthy hero.

As I mentioned in an earlier chapter, it was the Carlists who first asked for an Irish Brigade. They suggested that in the event of a brigade materialising it should fight side by side with the Requetes. General Franco decided that our brigade should be attached to the Tercio (legion), a tribute indeed which we all appreciated. The leadership of the Tercio could not appeal to Irishmen, however, as did the leadership of the Requetes. The ideals of the latter were more akin to our own. When we did become associated on the La Maranosa front, it was not surprising that the bonds of friendship became at once apparent; before long I was requested by some of my officers to take steps to have the Irish bandera attached to the Requetes.

Rev. Juan Alonso, S.J., was chaplain to the Requetes in our sector, and a particular favourite with our boys. He was an apt student of English, and with the knowledge of Spanish which the Irish were rapidly acquiring, they were able to make themselves understood. Each morning he celebrated Mass in the trenches, and our troops off duty were privileged to receive Holy Communion. On many occasions I heard the whistle of the shells over his head as he stood in front of his dugout, the Missal resting on a rock while he read the Mass in the open, with the Spanish blue sky as a canopy.

His was a noble manifestation of the Faith. He slept in a dugout on the front line, endured the hardships of the troops, shared all their risks. No wonder he was beloved by our Irish troops. Writing from Artillery Ridge, Madrid, on April 24th, 1937, to Captain P. Quinn of Kilkenny, Father Alonso said:

"I desire that the echo of my voice fills the corners of Ireland.

"When I arrived at the Artillery Ridge, to administer spiritual aid to the 'Red Caps' of the Tercio of Christ the King, I wished to view the panorama which extended before my eyes.

"To the north, Madrid, 'the big pond', as a famous novelist once described it, a title never better merited than in those days of Bolshevist infamy, which has made of the Spanish capital a marsh of crimes and corruption.

"To the east, the Jarama, which slowly meanders along, as if refusing the embrace of the Mazanares, fertilising the valley which was the theatre of a big battle, where the Muscovite terror sank down under the onslaught of the Spanish cavalry. To the west, the Hill of Angels, the hiding place of many sacred relics. To the south—the 15th Irish Catholic bandera.

"My liking for the Irish began the day in which the life of Father Doyle, S.J., fell into my hands. Through its pages, I saw the Catholicity and heroism of those fair-complexioned youths, and I have had the deepest satisfaction in seeing confirmed, in this holy war, these two most noble qualities—the sincere fervour and recollection with which they attended the Holy Sacrifice, approached the Eucharistic Table, and recited the Rosary. This inflamed my spirit and was the cause of admiration to the Requetes and Spanish officers.

"The respect and esteem of the Irish troops for their chaplain is something unusual in these countries. They built my dugout—church—with such promptitude of spirit and enthusiasm, just as if they were about to honour an angel. They always greeted me with respect and a pleasant smile. I lived with them as I did among my own friends; and every morning when I elevated the Immaculate Host in my sacerdotal hands I rejoiced in thinking that from the Glorified Wounds of Jesus Christ there mystically bursts forth His Redeeming Blood, filling the good hearts of the Catholic Irish.

"They are happy and playful, just like children, in time of leisure, valiant in battle, religious in their exercises of piety. Oh, may their remembrance be eternal in my soul.

"From the first day I was charmed with their company. The Irish and the Requetes passed their hours of rest together very enjoyably; they played, sang, and danced, with boyish chatter and laughter, some even now sport the red Carlist cap.

"Thinking of the strong and happy group of fair Irish and their red berets, I unconsciously think of the wheat-fields of Castile sprinkled with poppies.

"They go to Ireland, but their memory will live always in our hearts. Long live the Irish Catholic bandera."

On the day we left Maranosa Father Alonso wrote:

"Unforgettable Irishmen.

"You are going to your dear and Catholic Ireland, doing the miracle of going, and at the same time remaining here. You leave our land, but you stay in my Spanish heart.

"Profound gratitude to all the Irish officers, N.C.O.'s and legionaires I met on the Madrid hills. For ever I will remember with pride the fair and good Irishmen—fair like the Castilian wheat-fields, and good like the bread."

Captain Tyrrell O'Malley, Knight of Malta, of Ross House, Co. Mayo, gives the following account of a conversation he had on the French-Spanish frontier with Captain Grijalba, who fought side by side with the Irish Brigade at La Maranosa and described this front as "the worst spot near Madrid":

"I asked him: 'Have you met any of the Irish soldiers down there?'

"'The Irish', he answered. 'Why, yes; they are with me day after day and week after week in the trenches; never a rest. I myself did not change my clothes for fifty-seven days.'

"'And as soldiers?' I asked.

"He, thinking I was English and Pink, answered:

"'They are simply marvellous soldiers, marvellous, marvellous! So brave, and wonderful shots. They are completely trained men now.

"'They live on nothing and stand any weather. I remember one night when we were all dead tired. I found when visiting the sentries that all were sort of taking cover in the rain, snow and hail; but when I got near the Irish I saw them there, their sentries alert and upright and on the watch.

"'We Spaniards with them love them. It is so amusing to hear them and us praying at night, and then we are such friends. Oh! they are simply wonderful men and the bravest of the brave.'"

Chapter XVI

NATIONALIST SPAIN

TRAVELLING tens of thousands of miles in Spain during this
period, I saw most of the country that was under Nationalist control.

I found it necessary to travel regularly from the front to
Cáceres, always eager for news of another landing from Ireland,
to relieve our sorely tried men in the trenches. I also visited General Franco's headquarters at Salamanca and General Mola's
headquarters at Valladolid pretty frequently. My car indeed
became so well known that in all the miles I travelled I was not
"held up" once except to be warned of danger ahead. The
Felange were chiefly responsible for control of the roads, involv-
ing the scrutiny of *salvo conductoes*—the travelling permits, and
I must record my appreciation of the courtesy they invariably
showed to me, and to those who travelled with me. Everywhere
we were greeted with "*Viva Irlanda.*"

Evidence of war was on all sides, battered towns, charred
lorries and cars lying by the wayside, shell-holed roads, railways
out of use, and in general a trail of ruin and destruction. In some
towns, however, the only building destroyed was the Catholic
church, and on our making enquiries in such places it would be
discovered that invariably the only outrage committed was the
murder of the priest. Where the people were overwhelmingly

pro Franco, the few local Reds just burned the church and killed the priest before a hurried departure to join the Red army.

In Nationalist Spain life goes normally on. Men cultivate their lands, raising food for their own depleted households and for the troops at the front, shepherds lead their flocks to pasture, business is almost "as usual" in cities and towns. Peace rests on the hills and plains, disturbed only by the far-away booming of the guns—a reminder of the storm that has passed. Through the Press and the wireless, the Reds have succeeded in misrepresenting these facts. Books have been written on the war in Spain by people, many of whom never have been there.

The fact speaks for itself, that no person residing in the territory under Franco's control has had his life threatened and been obliged to go into exile. In the hotels in Nationalist Spain, France, Portugal, and even in England, there are many Spanish refugees from Red territory; but travel where you may, you will meet no refugees from the area occupied by Franco's forces. Notwithstanding the propaganda with which the Reds are so well served, not one outrage attributed to Franco's troops has been substantiated.

The story of the shooting of nine thousand workers after the capture of Seville has long since been exploded. General Queipo de Llano, by clever tactics, took Seville without firing a shot, the young men of the city having offered him their services. "The Massacre of Badajoz" is another splendid piece of fiction conceived by a journalist who had never been there. His message read: "As fast as they were captured the defending Government troops were executed in mass killings against the walls of the Cathedral. Blood ran in streams from the pavement, and two militia men were killed facing the high altar." This news appeared under the name of one of America's most reliable journalists, Mr. Packard, who denied all responsibility, and wrote contradicting the whole story. On investigation it transpired that Mr. Packard's name had been used in order to impress readers with the genuineness of the report. That is just typical of the propagandà flashed throughout the world in an effort to discredit the Nationalist cause, and of the "sensational news" which has been devoured in America and England. I had the pleasure of meeting Mr. Packard often: he is most conscientious, and not the type of journalist given to writing "scare" stories.

It is true that there have been many executions on the Nationalist side, but only after conviction by military courts, the personnel of which consists largely of experienced Judges.

How different are the conditions in Red Spain.

Mr. Arthur Bryant, the biographer of Earl Baldwin, writing in the *Observer*, has some comments to make upon the position there.

"Red Spain," he says, "is not a constitutional democracy. It is an inferno. Since July, 1936, some 350,000 non-combatants, men, women and children, living helplessly in that part of the Iberian Peninsula subject to the rule of what is euphemistically called the València Government, have been butchered in cold blood, under conditions of indescribable horror. At the same time, it is of interest to observe that, in the three-quarters of the Peninsula which is known as Nationalist Spain there is peace and security for all. No British citizen in Nationalist Spain has yet appealed for the assistance of the British Navy to effect his escape."

During an uneventful few days of the Irish bandera's stay in Ciempozuelos, I visited Seville, and was present for part of the Holy Week ceremonies there. It was an interesting experience.

During the "Republican" regime, the time-honoured Holy Week processions had been banned, but in 1937, with General Queipo de Llano in undisputed control, not only of the city of Seville, but of the country from the Portuguese border on the west to Granada on the east, and from the Mediterranean on the south to Cordova on the north, the beautiful ceremonies commemorating the Passion were renewed, and now with even more intense fervour.

All business is suspended from noon each day, and the whole population participate. Men, many barefooted, women with black veils, and never ending lines of children march through the streets many times daily, all through the week. Heavy platforms bearing large figures of the Redeemer, of His Sorrowful Mother, of the patron saints of Spain, and thousands of frames laden with those lovely flowers for which Andalucia is noted, are carried. It is a most remarkable demonstration and brings home to one how intense was the agony these good people must have endured when God's ministers and nuns were publicly mutilated, when the tabernacles were violated and the churches razed to the ground, probably by some of those who only a few years before had marched in these processions.

I called on Cardinal Ilundain, Archbishop of Seville, who received me in his humble abode with tears in his eyes. He spoke feelingly of Ireland, and said he thanked God he had lived to preside once again at the Holy Week ceremonies in his beloved Seville. The Cardinal died shortly afterwards—of a broken heart, it seemed.

I met also General Queipo de Llano, whose voice is heard so often on the air that he is known as the "Radio General." After Franco and Mola he has been recognised as the greatest general of the revolution. He commands the Southern army. The Red Government at the outset relied on his support, as he favoured a republican form of Government, but he was neither Communist nor Anarchist. Having assumed that the southern capital was being held for them by de Llano, the Government's dismay was great when he announced that he was holding Seville and the province of Andalucia for Franco. The Southern army followed their General practically to a man, with the result that Seville and the neighbouring towns escaped destruction, and there was very little loss of life. The General expressed the wish that the Irish Brigade should be attached to his command, but owing to the small numbers we were able to bring to Spain the question never materialised.

On my arriving in Seville the first to greet me had been Sancho Dávila, the enthusiastic young chief of the Felange for Southern Spain. He insisted I should remain a day extra to inspect the organisation at the Felange headquarters in Seville which controlled about 150,000 members, about one-half of whom were then engaged on the battle fronts, on railway and bridge protection duty, road patrolling and in garrisoning towns and villages. The remainder were undergoing courses of intensive training.

The Felange are unpaid, and provide their own commissariat, uniform, equipment and transport. Such perfect organisation I had not seen before; it was carried out with clock-like regularity, and every detail was provided for.

It was believed at the time of my visit to Seville that at least a second Irish bandera would succeed in getting to Spain almost immediately. A cordial invitation was extended to me to bring this bandera to Seville for training, and the choice of any barracks in the city was offered. The Felange officers were most enthusiastic in the matter, and actually secured General de Llano's approval. I received a similar invitation from Manuel Hedilla of Burgos, then chief of the Felange organisation of all Spain, for an Irish bandera to go to Burgos for training.

I was shown over Seville's huge aerodrome by the Marquis of Merito, and was taken for short flights over the city in a Junker bombing plane, and a Fiat fighter: in actual fighting the former is always supported by the latter.

I was the guest of the Duke of Algeciras at his home in Jerez, where the Duchess resides with their three little children. The Duke and his brother, the Marquis of Merito, are joint manufacturers of the famous Merito sherry and brandy and are among the largest wine producers in Spain. Owing to the popularity of the family, the vineyards and factories were not interfered with during the war, for the loyalty of the employees is a fine feature of the establishment. The Duke was the sixth nobleman in Spain during the days of King Alfonso, and the Duchess' father was Minister of the Interior during the dictatorship of Primo de Rivera.

It was fortunate for me that the Duke was selected to act as liaison officer between General Franco and myself. His judgment and his loyalty were invaluable to me; indeed, I would have found it difficult to get along without him, and I shall ever feel under a debt of gratitude to him. It is of interest that the Duke's forebears were Irish—his mother being a Garvey from Galway. He is now Adjutant to General Cabanellas, who was the first President of the Nationalist Government, and at present Inspector General of the Army. The General inspected our bandera before it left for the front, and spoke of it in high terms of praise.

The Duke's brother, the Marquis of Merito, is Adjutant to General Kindelán, recently appointed Minister for Air in the Nationalist Cabinet, whose ancestors were from Co. Meath. The Marquis himself is a distinguished aviator, and was amongst those who flew to the Canary Islands, and brought back General Franco to lead the revolt.

Chapter XVII

MOVEMENTS AND ORGANISATIONS IN SPAIN — THE BASQUES — THE MOORS — ANARCHISM — THE SPANISH WORKERS — THE CHURCH IN SPAIN

DURING my nine months stay in Nationalist Spain it was my privilege to come in contact with all the groups and many of the leaders; to get a grasp of the growth of events which brought about the appalling tragedy of that great Catholic land and with such knowledge to form a fair judgment of the situation so shamelessly misrepresented by newspaper propaganda.

In earlier chapters I have referred on the one hand to the Communist plan, as initiated and organised by Soviet agencies, and on the other hand to those movements which, though differing in many respects in matters relating to policy, represent all that is best in the national life of the country, their common allegiance being to faith and fatherland, their common object to stem the wave of godless materialism which was sweeping over the country, eating into the very hearts and souls of the factory workers and peasants. They were confronted with the terrific onslaught of militant atheism and intensive Russian propaganda which threatened to uproot the very fundamentals of Christian civilisation and Catholic culture, and to replace these according to plan by Anarchism and libertine Communism.

In this chapter I shall allude to other movements and groups not hitherto mentioned or only briefly referred to.

That the Basques—Catholics for the most part—allied themselves with the avowed destroyers of their religion and all the traditions held most sacred by them, has caused much confused thinking in Ireland and has been seized as a weapon to use against the Nationalist cause. It has been said that the Basques are as much entitled to complete independence from Spain as the Irish are to independence from England. But there is no similarity. The Basques are no more entitled to partition from Spain than six counties of Ulster are to partition from Ireland. Their claim is equally absurd.

I, too, misunderstood the position at first and in the agreement as to conditions of service for the Irish Brigade signed by General Franco and myself I had the following clause inserted:

"Clause Six.—The Irish Brigade may be employed on any front with the sole exception of the Basque front. General O'Duffy objects to the Irish troops being engaged against the Basque Nationalists for reasons of religion and traditional ties between the Basques and the Irish."

The Basque Country—the highlands of Spain—embraces four provinces: Navarra, Vizcaya, Guipuzcoa and Alava. The population of these provinces for the most part are of the same blood, speak the same language, and have manners and customs peculiar to themselves. Down through history, from the wars with the Moors in the eighth and ninth centuries to the days of the Spanish wars with England, the Basques fought to preserve a united Spain, of which they regarded themselves as an integral part—one in religion, one in history, one in a collective soul. They fought for exactly what Franco is fighting for now.

It was only when the Republican Government came into office, and began a war against religion that the Basque people, known to be deeply religious, adopted a definite separatist policy. The Soviet agents were not slow to take advantage of this opportunity to weaken the Spanish nation. The separatist policy of the Basques must be encouraged, the separatist policy of the Catalans must be encouraged. Soviet agents receive such instructions everywhere. Whatever the past record of the local Communist leaders, they must align themselves with the most advanced patriotism. In Ireland, professed Communists, who never raised a hand for Ireland in the Anglo-Irish war, now pose as most ardent patriots; they have been ordered to adopt that role. As the Spanish Hierarchy point out in their letter to the Bishops of the world—the Basques ignored the voice of the Church and became victims of the Red policy of throwing Catholics into the struggle, one against another.

According to plan, the Red Government offered the Basques political independence, and to use the words of Gil Robles, the great Catholic leader of Spain: "They then threw themselves into the arms of the Communists, they have not been loath to sell their beliefs for the purchase of an illusory independence, they allied themselves with the enemies of Christianity in exchange for a chimera."

In the so-called general election, held immediately before the Spanish war broke out, the Basques aligned themselves with the Communists. After the elections, when the policy of the assassination of priests and the burning of churches was put into operation, not even one Basque deputy protested in Parliament. When the patriot, Calvo Sotelo, shortly before he was murdered by Red auxiliary police, proposed a vote of no confidence in the Government because of these outrages, the Basque deputies voted with the Government. They were there and then promised their independence. Historic Spain was to be dismembered. The Basques went so far as to proclaim that they were Basques first and Catholics afterwards.

It is, however, but fair to the Basques, as we have known them, to point out that only a minority have thrown in their lot with the Reds—only a proportion of two out of the four provinces. The other two Basque provinces, and particularly Navarra, have provided the backbone of Franco's army in

Northern Spain, and it was they who utterly routed the misguided Basques who were fighting with the Reds at the fall of
Bilbao.

General Franco never attacked the Basques as such. To save
Northern Spain from the Reds, it was necessary to defeat all the
groups opposing him there and linked together with the Popular
Front. It is true that Basque priests have been killed by the
Nationalist forces, but they were killed in the front-line trenches.
How could they escape? If there is one thing which perhaps
more than any other will endure to General Franco's credit for
all time, it is his humane treatment of Basques, who deserved
very little consideration from him. The siege of Bilbao lasted
many months. Not once during the siege did he bomb the city.
When it was about to fall, tens of thousands of citizens fled.
They were allowed to go in peace. Over 150,000 remained and
they were at once recognised and treated as good citizens by
General Franco's officers.

General Franco has made it perfectly clear in all his pro-
nouncements on National policy that his ideal is Spain one and
undivided. There can be no regional autonomy in a nation. It
leads to a disruption of national unity. He may give administra-
tive autonomy to the Basques and to Catalans so far as it does
not run counter to the unity of the Spanish nation, but he will
never agree to the partition of his country. It must be intact.

I learned on most reliable authority of the treatment meted
out by the Basques in Bilbao to several hundred Civil Guard
officers and men who surrendered in good faith to their former
friends and admirers, on condition that no ill would befall them.
For generations past the Civil Guards have by their exemplary
conduct, their impartiality, and their devotion to duty during
difficult times, endeared themselves to the Spanish people.

The surrendering Guards marched, under their officers, into
the plaza of Bilbao and handed up their arms to the Basque
authorities. No sooner had they done so than machine-gun fire
was opened upon them from positions previously occupied on

all sides of the plaza. In a few minutes seven hundred brave men lay dead on the square.

If there was nothing else, the account of this cold-blooded and treacherous slaughter of peace officers was sufficient to convince me that those Basques, who were fighting against the Nationalists, were little better than the Reds; at once I intimated to General Franco that I desired to have Clause Six expunged from the conditions of service of the Irish Brigade.

I met Basque priests when I was travelling through France to and from Spain, who were against General Franco. They seemed to be good priests, worthy of their sacred calling, but they failed to convince me that their alignment with the Communists was or could be justified from any point of view. To my mind if the Basques had joined with the bishops and priests and the Catholic people of Spain under Franco's banner, rather than under the banner of Caballero, they would have served their God and their country better.

Then there are the Moors. In my younger days I laboured under a very false impression that the Moors were savages, without culture or civilisation, and not until I went to Spain was the idea altogether dispelled. Much has been written by people who have never been to Spain, and who know little or nothing about the Moors, condemning the use of these African troops by General Franco; they forgot to mention that during the Great War both France and England used their coloured soldiers in defence of Catholic Belgium and of the freedom of small nations—including Ireland—as we were told at the time. France and England employed these negroes because they formed part of the regular fighting forces of their countries, and for precisely the same reason General Franco employs the Moorish troops in the Spanish war of liberation. Moreover, the Moors are Spanish citizens and are fighting in defence of God and their religion.

The Moors are not negroes; the shape of the head, nose, and mouth, their hair and eyes, are more characteristic of the European. Many Moors are fairer in colour than either the Italian or the Spaniard. They are splendid soldiers, brave, loyal, reliable and well-disciplined. Every member of the Irish Brigade can bear out my assertion that the Moors are not given to the torturing of prisoners, or to the other inhuman acts imputed to them in the Press. I would much prefer to find myself a prisoner of the Moors than of the Russian Ogpu. They are indeed a highly civilised people, whose culture has left its mark in Spanish literature, music and art. Some of the most exquisite architectural gems in Spain are their work, and many of Franco's Moorish troops today are the direct descendants of the famous Moorish families of Granada, Cordova and Seville.

The comradeship in arms between Spaniards and Moors is a national tradition. They admire a good leader, and in General Franco they have found their idol, whom they learned to respect when he commanded the foreign legion in Morocco. His bodyguard is composed entirely of Moors; they accompany him wherever he goes, and he could not have a better escort.

Again, the Moors constitute only a small proportion of the Nationalist forces—a much smaller proportion than that of Russians in the Red army of Spain—and few will urge that the average Moor is less civilised than the average Russian. The Red Government, I may say, tried all it could to induce the Moors to take its side, but failed. The Moors have a deep piety and will fight against anyone who attacks religion. The burned churches and the murder of priests infuriated them. "Bad men those Reds. We kill them for they destroyed the holy women of God."

I was invited to a reception given in Cáceres to the Grand Vizier, or chief Moorish priest of Spanish Morocco—a distinguished-looking, refined and highly educated man. Our Irish pipers were called in to play a selection of Irish airs during the function, and made a strong impression on the Grand Vizier. When called on to reply to the toast of his health, he said: "I would prefer to listen to the stimulating music of the Irish pipers, and to look on those fine men marching up and down the room in their beautiful national costumes, than to make a speech." Speaking then of the Irish Brigade he said: "Why does a little island, far away—holy Ireland—send its volunteers to fight for Franco? It is for the same reason that the Moors are fighting here. We are fighting," he answered with emotion, "against those who deny God".

Next day the Grand Vizier visited the various hospitals in southern Spain where the wounded Moorish troops were being treated. He requested that the Irish pipers' band should accompany him to play for the wounded, and he introduced me to the patients saying: "Ireland here, too, for the same cause."

The Moorish troops were particularly friendly to the Irish troops, and they could recount traditional tales of the bravery and dash of the Irish soldiers of other days, in old Seville and Granada. The Reds nicknamed the Irish Brigade "the Catholic Moors", which was intended as an insult but regarded by us as a compliment. We found the Moors polite, generous and hospitable.

Accompanying the Moorish troops one invariably finds a following of Moorish "merchants" selling all sorts of things—jewellery, highly-coloured scarfs and ties, toffee, chocolate, etc. The Irish were their best customers. When the Moorish troops were called into action, however, those "merchants" at once discarded their merchandise, picked up rifles and joined their fighting comrades. Their desire to fight the Reds exceeded far their desire to make a few pesetas.

It is believed that after the war General Franco will grant a generous measure of autonomy to the Moors in Spanish Morocco. No race deserves it more, and none is better fitted to govern itself.

Spain would now appear to be the centre of world anarchism. Barcelona publishes anarchist papers daily and weekly, and there are also monthly periodicals. Anarchism, of course, is opposed to Communism, which stands for some form of Government, as in Russia. In Spain it would appear that the Anarchists and Communists are co-operating, but the Anarchists are really the controlling factor.

Anarchism means the negation of government. The anarchist is opposed to organised society in every shape and form. He is opposed to any form of central authority, and is therefore opposed to God from whom all authority is derived. The Church and the State, the two bulwarks of society, must be destroyed, for, according to him, on these two great foundations rests the whole capitalist system. The anarchist motto is: "Neither God nor master, neither faith nor law."

Anarchism is summed up by the Most Rev. Dr. Fogarty, Bishop of Killaloe, when he says: "Its aim is to destroy all authority, to make men like creatures of the wilds. In pursuance of that policy the Anarchists clearly realise that the first authority to be dealt with is the Church; hence it is the first part of their programme to pull down and destroy the Church of Christ."

The Communists believe in a "government of the proletariat", or a workers' republic. They differ from the Anarchists in that respect, but are at one with them in hatred of Christ and His Church; on the question of common ownership; in the suppression of all individual effort and enterprise; and in the doctrine that marriage and the family are artificial institutions.

The Soviet Minister for Education says: "We hate Christians. The best of them are our worst enemies. They preach love of one's neighbour, which is contrary to our principles. Down with love of one's neighbour, what we want is hate. We have dealt with the Kings of the earth, let us now deal with the Kings of the sky."

These are the aims and policies of the major forces against which General Franco is fighting—the forces responsible for the terrible tragedy of Spain.

Of Spanish "trade unions" it should be understood that they have not the remotest similarity to Irish or British trade unions. They are not really workers' unions at all, but powerful political Jewish-Masonic organisations, directed and financed by the Communist International. They were brought into existence, not for the benefit of the worker, but for the sole purpose of destroying organised Christian society. They were known as the

C.G.T. (Communist), the C.N.T. (Direct Action), and the F.A.I. (Federación Anarquista Ibérica). These organisations supplied the "brigades" which carried out most of the dreadful crimes I have referred to in previous chapters.

It is to such organisations that the British and French trade unions have been sending material aid since the outbreak of hostilities. They would have us believe that these were trade unions in the strict sense of the word, whose members were honest workers, fighting to overthrow a capitalist system, with all its abuses.

The only genuine workers' organisations in Spain before the war were the Spanish Christian Workers' Syndicates. They were organised on Christian lines, so when the revolution broke out membership involved the death penalty. In Spain, as elsewhere, Communists and Anarchists loathe *bona fide* trade unions.

The bogus trade unions were used by the Red Government from the outset. Moscow ordered the revolution to take place in July, 1936, beginning with the execution of all the leaders of the opposition. As a "reprisal" for the execution of these leaders, feint attacks were to be made on trade union headquarters all over the country simultaneously. The trade unions would then reply with a general strike and occupy Government offices.

The premature murder of Calvo Sotelo by the police upset the scheme. New plans had to be evolved, and these were forestalled at the very last moment by a spontaneous rising of the people behind General Franco, who in a few weeks was in control of more than half the country.

Long before war broke out, the bogus workers' unions had practically ruined the agricultural industry. Farmers were forced to pay agricultural labourers thirty pesetas (15/-) per day for four hours work, a figure which was estimated at fifty per cent, more than the value of the product itself, when rent, taxes, cost of the seed and fertilisers were taken into account. The result was that the farmers handed over the crops to their farm hands, and in many cases the crops rotted in the ground. The unions then secured authority from the Government to sell the farmer's cattle and to cut down and carry off his trees. Many farmers who protested were murdered, and the murderers were not even arrested, much less convicted.

"The Catholic Church in Spain is immensely wealthy, the clergy are rolling in riches and the Jesuits own most of the industrial concerns, while the worker starves. In order to maintain its wealth the Church has allied itself with the grandees and the wealthy capitalist classes against the down-trodden masses and the landless ill-paid worker."

These are some of the calumnies which Communist propaganda levels against the Catholic Church in Spain. Even in Ireland I do not think I was even once in a discussion on Spain in which the questions of the "fabulous wealth of the Church", and the "priest-ridden Spanish people" were not raised.

Anyone who has been to Spain, or who has studied the history of the Church there, will realise at once how utterly false and ridiculous these charges are. It is true that there are some magnificent churches in the larger cities, and centuries-old priceless treasures—paintings, vestments, gold chalices, monstrances, and so on, but these are national property, and both canon and civil law forbid alienation. Even if they wished it the clergy could not dispose of this property, and it does not satisfy the pangs of hunger to gaze on the grandeur of such ecclesiastical buildings, or the loveliness of such paintings. We might as well say that our soldiers are wealthy, because we see imposing military parades, or that our doctors are wealthy because we have well-equipped hospitals.

There are splendid cathedrals in Spain, but more than half the churches are very old structures, tottering to decay, many located in the back streets of the towns and practically without furniture. It would be impossible to brighten them. How different it is in Ireland where we can be proud of those beautiful churches we see everywhere, especially in the rural areas.

The residences of the Bishops are for the most part simple and plain in contrast with the houses surrounding, and the poorest house in the towns and villages I have seen is that occupied by the parish priest. In some cases he has only a single room, and the value of the furniture does not exceed a few pounds. The Bishops do not possess motor cars, and the priests cannot even afford the luxury of pedal bicycles. The parishes are large and scattered, but the priests ordinarily have to get along on foot; they are badly dressed, and generally it is at once impressed on one that the parish priest is the poorest, though the most deserving person, in the community.

During the past hundred years the Church in Spain had been gradually deprived of all its property. The Government made a Concordat with the Holy See in which the latter validated the State's claim to the property, on condition that provision would be made for the support of the hierarchy, clergy, churches, convents, schools and charitable institutions. A sum of £5,400,000 was agreed on to cover all. Four thousand parish priests were to receive an allowance of £20 each per annum, seven thousand to receive £30, three thousand £40, two hundred £80, fifty £100, and lay-brothers from £5 to £30 each.

In the annual Budget, however, this altogether inadequate allowance was reduced year by year, and by 1916 the sum voted for all Church purposes had fallen from £5,400,000 to £1,668,000.

Out of miserable pittances the clergy were forced to pay income tax, deducted at the source and much higher in proportion than that paid by Civil Servants. The pay of an ordinary clerk in the Civil Service was higher than that of the best-paid parish priest. In brief, the Spanish clergy were the worst paid and the most highly taxed body in the State.

Then it was alleged that the Spanish priest was able to supplement his salary by Mass stipends, and so on. In Ireland the Church is supported thus by the people, the chief sources of revenue being offerings, dues, donations, stole fees and stipends, but such sources of income are practically unknown to the Spanish clergy. It is a rare thing for a priest to receive a stipend for a Mass in Spain, nor does he seek it. The Bishop and priests in Cáceres were much impressed by the generosity of all ranks of the Irish Brigade in this respect.

Stole fees for marriages and baptisms range in Spain from ten pence to a maximum of four shillings, and church collections were not permitted until General Franco took control. I observed, too, that while the Irish officers considered a peseta (five pence)—not too generous, the Spaniards' usual donation—even with well-to-do people—was a penny.

The allowances of the Hierarchy ranged from £400 per annum to £1,600 in the case of the Cardinal Primate. Out of this allowance the Bishop maintained his own household, contributed to the upkeep of seminaries, churches, convents, and was expected to pay to all charities, and to bestow alms generously.

In marked contrast were the salaries voted to themselves by the Ministers of State. The President, for example, received in salary and expenses the sum of £12,800 per annum, and the other Ministers were paid in proportion. Each Minister received for valet and other personal services, more than the allowance granted to the Cardinal Primate of Spain for all purposes. The Mayors of Barcelona and Madrid each received £3,000 per annum in salary and allowances.

These are the Ministers and other officials of the Republic who led in the campaign of lying about the "vast riches" of the Church in Spain.

British newspapers have joined in this propaganda campaign, conveniently ignoring the fact that the Anglican Primate of England has a salary ten times as great as that of the Primate of Spain, and that on an average the Anglican Bishop receives a salary four times as great as the Spanish Bishop.

And miserable as the allowances to the Spanish clergy were, the Republican Government, on coming into office in 1931, decreed that all State aid for the Church should end. Their predecessors had confiscated all Church property and made an allowance in lieu thereof; the Republican Government not only held on to the property, but dishonoured the Concordat. The clergy were thus left without any provision whatever. The answer of the Government to criticism was: "If you want priests you can pay for them."

It was the religious Orders, particularly the Jesuits, who were subjected to the most vicious propaganda—their wealth was immense; it was said they owned the principal industrial concerns, they had huge investments, and their schools were run for mercenary purposes. Again the most superficial examination shows at once how untrue are these allegations.

Even before the State seized her property, the Church enjoyed only the use of it, and she exercised that use solely for the benefit of the Spanish people. In most cases the property that was confiscated represented voluntary gifts to the Church. The State ruthlessly disregarded the intentions of the donors.

The Jesuits did not engage in industry. It was not and is not their vocation. The only "business concerns" they had were the leper asylums, for the upkeep of which they were obliged to beg and preach. Their investments were subject to Canon Law restrictions and the interest was barely sufficient to provide for the sons of the poor who were novices for the priesthood. The Azaña Government were forced to admit when they took over the clerically-run schools that not one of them had been paying its way. It was found too, after confiscation, that the property used by the Jesuits was heavily in debt, and that they had been struggling hard to pay the interest on the loans. While the Government were prating about social justice, enjoying their big salaries and doing nothing to develop the social life of the workers, the priests were doing all they could within their very limited resources to improve conditions, and organisations for Catholic workers were established over the country, to spread the teachings of the Church on social justice.

When, however, the individual clergy in Spain had barely sufficient to keep body and soul together, when the Church as a body had neither the funds nor the influence to direct education on Christian lines, and the State suppressed the teaching Orders, the youth of Spain became an easy victim to Bolshevist propaganda.

If we except the peaceful and progressive period of the Primo de Rivera administration, we need have no hesitation in saying that for some years previous to 1931 the Spanish Governments were almost as guilty as the Governments since for the present tragedy of Spain; nor can His Catholic Majesty Alfonso XIII be absolved from a share of the guilt.

The Church in Spain has been cruelly treated by the State for generations past, and it has recently endured a martyrdom not surpassed in the days of Nero, or in the penal days in Ireland. The Christian world has confidence that the success of the arms of General Franco will ensure that its sublime sacrifice is not in vain. He has said: "We shall make a special point of restoring the churches and we shall see that the clergy are provided with appropriate means to carry out their spiritual task. Our State is to be a Catholic State, for the true Spain has been, is now, and will be Catholic."

FRANCO — PRIMO DE RIVERA — GIL ROBLES

G ENERAL Francisco Franco Bahamonde is one of the greatest men I have ever met. I do not make the statement idly,
for I have, during my travels, met and in some instances have
known closely many of the world's greatest men, French, Italian, German and British statesmen, three Presidents of the
United States, and, of course, all the Irish statesmen.

It was my privilege to be in continual contact with General
Franco over a period of some eight or nine months. I saw in him
the embodiment of all Spain's traditionally splendid culture—
religious, civil and military.

He was courtly. My first meeting with him occurred when
he had decided at the last moment against bringing the Brigade
from Ireland, because of his hopes for a real Non-Intervention
Pact. A dictator in all the circumstances of war would have told
me curtly that he had decided against the proposal and dismissed me. The military importance of the Brigade, as I have
already indicated, was slight; it represented then in military
terms only a few thousand men at most, whose transport from
a smallish island remote from Spain by many hundreds of miles
would be attended with difficulty and expense. General Franco,
with the most delicate courtesy, went to considerable trouble to

explain to me the international difficulties of the problem confronting him, and how inadvisable it would be to bring the Brigade at that stage.

As his extraordinary career shows, and as I have myself seen, he inspires the devotion of every man under his command. When he goes to a front where an advance must be made, as he usually does, and assumes local control, the Nationalist soldiers become invincible.

His conduct of the war, in all its phases, shows military genius, which is unrivalled today. His strategy is brilliant, and his leadership perfect. Yet he has no dictatorial ambitions. He wants to see Spain powerful and happy, but he is not a politician, he is not attached to any "ism", he makes no speeches, and he avoids a public demonstration like a plague.

He is a genuinely devout Catholic. He makes no pretensions, he does not beat his breast piously in public, but his sense of duty to God and to the Church and to his country is complete.

General Franco was born forty-five years ago in Galicia, the home of many Irishmen in the past. His father was a naval officer, holding the position of Commandant of the naval base at Ferrol.

Faith is a tradition with his family. His mother, who was a Bahamonde, belonged to an old Catholic Galician family. In the village where she was born a cross was erected by her father, many years ago, which bears the inscription: "This Cross was planted here by Juan Bahamonde so that his fellow-townsmen may remember their Faith." It is fitting that General Franco is today raising the standard so that Spain and the world may remember their Faith.

At the early age of fourteen Franco entered the Spanish Infantry College, where he had a brilliant course, and on passing out he volunteered, like his colleague Mola, for service in Morocco. His promotion was rapid. At twenty he was captain of a company and three years later he was promoted on the field to the rank of major.

He was always a keen student of military science and history as well as a brave soldier, and when Colonel, now General, Millán-Astray was entrusted with the formation of the Tercio (legion) in 1921, he had the young major appointed his second in command. It is not surprising that the Tercio should have become the cream of the Spanish army with such officers in command.

General Millán-Astray, whom I always met when visiting Salamanca, is one of the most romantic military figures in Spain. He has been wounded in action several times, has lost an eye and an arm, but is as keen and full of vitality as ever. He was a warm friend of the Irish bandera.

Before he was a year in the Tercio Major Franco was awarded the Military Medal, one of the highest awards in the gift of the Spanish army, and in 1923, at the age of thirty, he was given command of the Tercio, with the rank of Colonel.

Following the murder of the Cardinal Archbishop of Saragossa by the anarchists in 1923 General Primo de Rivera formed a Military Directory and suspended Parliament. Recognising the ability of Colonel Franco, who had now won his second Military Medal, de Rivera brought him back from Morocco, raised him to the rank of Brigadier-General, and entrusted him with the training of the army's officer personnel. Franco founded the Military Academy of Saragossa, which soon attracted the attention of military experts throughout Europe.

Primo de Rivera's Directory lasted eight years, and was the most peaceful and prosperous period that Spain had enjoyed for a long time. Travelling through the country today, one can see on all sides evidence of the remarkable achievements and reforms he effected. It is almost inconceivable that any statesman could effect so much in so short a time.

He brought to a successful conclusion the long-drawn-out campaign in Spanish Morocco, he made peace with the Moors, he reformed the army and the social services—in a word, he transformed the whole Spanish administration. He dealt effectively with those who aimed at destroying the Church and overthrowing the Monarchy. He cleansed the cities of immorality, he opened up the remote parts of Spain by the construction of new railways, he utilised the water power of the rivers for industrial purposes, and he initiated a scheme of irrigation on a wide scale. Again, few countries today can boast of a better laid-out main road system than Spain. The road signs are so skilfully designed that one could scarcely lose one's way, the distances are marked down to the tenth of a kilometre, every incline, bend, cross-road, and school is indicated—in short, it is a pleasure to travel by the Spanish roads, notwithstanding the mountainous nature of the country. All this is the work of Primo de Rivera, and in addition he established a chain of controlled first-class hotels throughout the rural parts, to appeal to the tourist.

He tackled vigorously the question of absentee landlordism, and sought to remedy the grievances of the tenants. His agricultural policy, more than anything else perhaps, led to his downfall, as it united the grandees, aristocrats and the extensive landowners against him. King Alfonso sided with them against de Rivera, and, I was told, interfered to the detriment of most of his schemes for reform.

De Rivera was too timid to assert himself against this formidable combination. Not possessing the forcefulness of a Mussolini, he yielded to pressure, retired, went into exile, and died in a short time from a broken heart.

As I was travelling through Spain, I heard nothing but the highest praise of the de Rivera administration, and the opinion was everywhere expressed that had he continued in control the country would have been spared the tragedy of today. The day of his downfall was an evil one for Spain, and when the King—who was held largely responsible for it—fled from the country himself only a short time afterwards, there was little sympathy for him anywhere, inside or outside of Spain.

The army could possibly have saved Primo de Rivera, but General Franco adopted a neutral attitude and said: "We must put the country first; soldiers must stand aside from politics, and think only of the nation." When afterwards the Republic was proclaimed Franco's reward was to have his great Military Academy closed down, and to be deprived of command. For two years he was without a post.

The election of 1933 having shown a decided swing towards the Right, Franco was given command of the Balearic Islands, and in 1934, when the miners' revolt broke out in the Asturias, the Republican Government was constrained to call upon him to come to its rescue. He was successful, and after two weeks restored law and order with the minimum loss of life. This time the Government was more grateful—he was given command of the army in Morocco. It was then that he found his way to the hearts of the Moors, an achievement which served him well in later years.

When Lerroux replaced Azaña as Prime Minister he made Gil Robles his Minister for War, who in turn appointed Franco to be Chief of the General Staff. Robles and Franco found the army split into several factions, and almost completely disorganised because of Communist intervention. Franco's job was not to create a military academy now, but to rebuild the army of the nation, and he threw his whole heart and soul into the task. He was determined that the army should serve the Republic as faithfully as it had served the Monarchy.

Gil Robles, a great Catholic and a great statesman, while a believer in the Monarchy, accepted the Republican form of government in the interests of peace, and did not spare himself to make it a success. He was leader of the biggest party in the Cortes by far, yet President Zamora persistently refused to invite him to form a Government. Robles at this time had the youth of the country behind him, he united the agricultural workers and the farmers' sons in a great Catholic union, and he was recognised by the overwhelming majority of the people as the hope of Spain. When his prestige was at its highest, when the Reds were disintegrated, he was implored to call out the army, and seize power. He refused, on the grounds that he had the nation with him, and that when the time came he would secure power by constitutional means. That time never came, however, for

Zamora was in league with the Communists, and fearing the growing popularity of Robles, he played into their hands and dissolved Parliament.

At once the youth of Spain fell away from Robles. They felt he had let them down in refusing to take over control when he was in a position to do so, having the country behind him, and they felt he was weak as Minister for War, in permitting the Communists to organise, drill and arm. A new organisation was formed—the Felange, and Robles' youthful followers flocked into this. Many of them today attribute the rise of Communism to his adherence to constitutional methods when confronted with a problem which threatened the nation.

Still, the result of the general election which followed the dissolution of the Cortes proved that Robles still had even yet the confidence of the majority of the people. I have shown in an earlier chapter how the Red minority was then converted into a majority. The new Government, however, removed Zamora from the Presidency—which he richly deserved—and placed Azaña, the present President, in office.

While Robles was certainly far too timid, it cannot be denied that he was honest and sincere, and were it not for Soviet intervention his policy would have succeeded. The new Spain cannot afford to do without a statesman of such ability. General Franco has a very high regard for him, and I have no doubt he will be called upon to assist in the reconstruction of the edifice of State.

The extreme Left now in control decided on a purge of the army. It was persecuted and humiliated, yet it remained loyal. It is known that Zamora, the President, was in a secret pact with the Communists and Anarchists to destroy it. Largo Caballero, when challenged on army policy, replied: "We will turn the generals into corporals, and the corporals into generals, if necessary." General Franco was sent to an unimportant command in the Canary Islands—an order which amounted practically to banishment—but he obeyed without a murmur.

When on July, 1936, Calvo Sotelo was murdered in Madrid by uniformed forces of the State, and when chaos and anarchy broke out over the country, Catholic Spain turned its eyes to the Canary Islands. If there was to be a movement, nobody doubted who would direct it.

On 17th July an aeroplane left for the Canary Islands bringing Spain's call to Franco. When convinced that there was no possible alternative he accepted, flew to Morocco, called the army into action, and it responded to a man. Soon all the best elements in the national life of Spain were flocking to the Nationalist cause with shouts of "Long live Christ the King," "*Viva España*," "*Viva* Franco," and at the end of two months General Franco was invested as head of the new Spanish State.

Chapter XIX

MOLA — THE NEW SPAIN

WHEN Franco was relegated to the Canary Islands, the late General Mola was sent to command a small body of troops in Pamplona. It was there he rose in consort with Franco in defence of the liberties of Spain.

Mola, an earnest Catholic, was one of the finest soldier-statesmen, one of the most patriotic and best beloved sons of Spain. Behind his stern features too there was kindness and good humour. Now he lies in the Carlist plot in Pamplona, in the province of Navarra, which he saved from the horrors of the civil war. The youth of the entire province rallied to his side and marched with him to meet Franco in his advance from the South.

Mola was born in Cuba in 1887. He was the son of an officer of the Civil Guard, and had his early training in the Military Academy of the Alcázar of Toledo. On passing out, like his younger colleague Franco, he sought service in Africa, and his principal training was carried out in the hard school of Moroccan warfare. During his seventeen years' campaigning in Morocco he held various posts and acquired knowledge which was later to stand him and his country in good stead. His promotion was almost as rapid as that of Franco. He was twice seriously wounded, and for distinguished service in the field was promoted captain in 1912, major in 1914, colonel in 1925 and

Brigadier-General in 1927. He won many military decorations, and when General Berenguer succeeded Primo de Rivera in the Military Directory, Mola was chosen for the difficult position of Chief of Police.

In the early years of the Republic, Mola, like Franco, was deprived of a command, but when Franco became Chief of Staff Mola served on his staff, and later was appointed in command of the military forces in Morocco. There he completed the work of winning over the Moors for Spain, which Franco had begun when occupying a similar position.

Mola's character and the Nationalists' vision of the new Spain can best be described by a declaration he made a few months before his death: "We shall create a great country, let there be no doubt of it; and we shall do so with the help of all and for the sake of all. Later, when the years have passed and the nightmare of war has faded, the historian will close the chapter of this bloody and glorious stage in the life of our nation with this expressive commentary: 'When the contest ceased a new State was built up on the ruins of a sorry past, and Spain once more became herself; the Spain of the Cid, of Ferdinand and Isabella, of Cortez, Pizarro, and the Golden Age of literature—immortal Spain.'"

Some people predict that Franco will be confronted with many difficulties in dealing with his own followers, when he has brought the conflict to a successful conclusion; that it will not be easy in peace time to reconcile the various groups, formerly more or less opposed to one another, which are now fighting together so harmoniously on the Nationalist side. I have had very close relations with all these groups and I do not share this view. I am convinced that the forebodings are based on a misunderstanding of the new and different Spain which the war has brought into being. I believe Spain will emerge resplendent from the shadows, its youth imbued with high ideals, and enkindled with a true nationalism.

The only groups sufficiently strong to create trouble, if they were disposed to do so, are the Felange and the Carlists, and they are not so disposed. It is very unlikely that any of the former forces in Spain will try to push themselves to the fore again. Franco too has provided against any such divisions by merging the Felange, the Carlists, and the Monarchists into one solid national organisation the "Falange Española Tradicionalista."

The Felange was founded in 1933 by José Antonio Primo de Rivera, eldest son of the former Premier. I spent a short holiday with him in 1934, and found he had a particular regard for Ireland, for private reasons. He was one of the first to be arrested by the Red Government and was executed.

The Felange are recruited mostly from the working classes and represent more than any other organisation the labour element in Spain. Their policy and programme are based on sound Catholic and national principles; they are anti-Liberal, anti-capitalist, opposed to the political party system of government, and have made big sacrifices in the war.

Some people oppose Franco under the pretence that the war in Spain is a fight between Fascism and Democracy and they have no use for Fascism. Nothing could be more absurd. If their reasoning is sound how can they account for the fact that the "democrats" fire on the Tabernacle, and challenge Christ if He is really present to come out and smite them. Why do these "democrats" remove the figures of Christ and Mary from the churches, and place them on the highways after having painted them immodestly? Is it that those who are not Communist are Fascist, and that as the Catholic Church condemns Communism, then the Church is Fascist?

The Requetes, whom I have described already, are imbued with all the high ideals of their forefathers. They are real knights of Christ and the Faith. They too are anti-Liberal, anti-capitalist, and opposed to the political party system of government. They favour a Corporate State within the Monarchy.

It appears that the system of government by the biggest political party in the State has gone for ever in Spain. There is need for a strong central authority for some years to consolidate the victory which has cost so much and to establish peace on a lasting basis. Very probably the provisional Government, or National Council, which Franco has created as a war-time measure, will be continued for a while to enable the country to settle down again to peace conditions. He does not favour a military dictatorship as I have said, and has often declared that it is not the duty of the army to rule but to defend the country.

Franco is planning for a new State, based on Spanish tradition, adapted to his country's peculiar needs, designed and governed on the teachings of the Papal Encyclicals on social justice. He is not likely to adopt any foreign model, but he may be influenced by the system in neighbouring and friendly Portugal, which is now accepted as the nearest approach to the ideal form of the vocational, as against the political party system of representative government. As a soldier Franco has led the world in the fight against Communism. Now as a statesman we may look to him to give a lead in the formation of an ideal State—Catholic not merely in name, but in spirit.

The republican form of government did not get a fair chance in Spain, because of the circumstances under which it was launched. The Communists and Anarchists, who were really in control, used the Ministers as puppets to make it appear for a time that their policy was constitutional. Presidents and Prime Ministers were no more to them than rubber stamps. Zamora had to make way for Azaña in the Presidency. Caballero—who called himself the Lenin of Spain—succeeded Giral as Prime Minister, and in turn had to make way for Negrin, the present Prime Minister. These men made no appeal to the patriotism of the better educated youth; eighty per cent, of Spanish students it should be observed are fighting on the Nationalist side. Long before the revolution the battle-cry was not "*Viva* Spain," but "*Viva* Russia." Paintings of great Spaniards of the past—soldiers and scholars, not to speak of saints—were replaced by paintings and pictures of Lenin and Stalin. Before the revolution and since, of course, Freemasonry has had a predominating influence in the Cabinet and Ministers put their obligations to the Order before their obligations to their country. It has been asserted on the highest authority in Spain, that Calvo Sotelo was murdered under orders received from the General Council of Freemasonry in Geneva, and that the Minister of the Interior, then Señor Barcia, carried these orders to Spain.

In my opinion a republican form of government does not suit the Spanish temperament, and I think there will be a restoration of the Monarchy after a time. Many people I met inside and outside the Army favour it, but I found no one to advocate the return of Alfonso, though there was much support for his third son, Don Juan. If the Monarchy is restored the King will probably be no more than a symbol; this would satisfy the Monarchists, the Felange would make no objection, and as the Carlists' heir presumptive has been killed in an accident abroad, leaving no issue, they, too, would probably agree to Don Juan.

The grandees will never again have the power they formerly wielded with the Sovereign. There will be no more privileges because of birth or position, and the days of absentee landlordism are gone forever in Spain. To a certain extent the grandees and landlords have been responsible for preparing the soil on which Communism flourished; many of them were not as just to the small tenant farmers as they should have been.

In the new Spain the workers will enjoy a charter unequalled in any country today. Already their social status has been raised, and the Nationalist State guarantees continuity of work for all. The number of working hours is limited, a minimum wage has been fixed, married women will no longer be employed in workshops or factories, there will be annual holidays with full pay for all workers, and Sundays and religious festivals are to be respected. The rights of private property of course are recognised and the family is regarded as the basis of society. All industries and technical professions are being organised in unions in which the employer and employee will be represented, and a fixed proportion of the profits must be devoted to the improvement of working conditions. The State will not interfere in industry, unless private enterprise appears to be misdirected.

A family wage fund has been organised, and is now in operation, whereby workers will receive extra wages in proportion to the size of their families.

Señora Franco has established social welfare clubs all over Spain. A feature of these is that no discrimination is shown—widows and orphans of those who fought for the Reds receive equal consideration with the victims of the Red terror.

One day each week—Monday—is known as *plato unico* (one plate) day. Usually there are five courses for dinner. On *plato unico* day only one course is served, but the diner pays for five. The profit goes to the social welfare clubs, and in this way everyone who dines in hotels, restaurants or boarding-houses contributes. In addition, a tax of ten per cent. is charged on all drinks served in cafés or bars, for the same good cause.

Special measures are provided to assist agricultural workers and fishermen, and each peasant family will have a plot of ground for itself. Happily, too, the 1937 harvest was the best on record, and the granaries overflowed.

Unemployment does not exist in Nationalist Spain today—either in the cities or the rural parts. The country has undergone a complete change. Normal conditions prevail in four-fifths of the land, and there is no evidence of force—Franco is not feared, he is beloved. He has not even found it necessary to raise a foreign loan. Nationalist Spain is financing the war of liberation itself, and it is noteworthy that although the peseta issued by the Red Government is supposed to have a heavy gold backing, its exchange value is only half that of the Franco peseta. No higher tribute could be paid to the efficiency of the system of exchange control exercised by the Nationalist Government.

At the beginning of the war, the Red Government seized all the gold in the Bank of Spain, amounting, it is estimated, to £90,000,000. A large sum was transferred to the Bank of France, and Russia is reported to have received £20,000,000 in gold pesetas in exchange for munitions of war. This was effected by Dr. Negrin, who was Finance Minister in Caballero's Cabinet and is now Prime Minister.

Adventurers made fortunes in these arms' deals. Franco's Navy, for instance, captured a ship conveying a cargo of arms from Russia to València. It was taken to Seville, where it was found that the guns were not only antiquated, but absolutely worthless.

The Spanish Government had no right to the gold in the Bank of Spain. It did not belong to them. The directors sent a protest to the various countries of Europe, giving particulars of the amounts seized; following this, some of them were murdered, and the others fled. The chief cashier of the Bank committed suicide. The Government then appointed nominees to the directorships declared "vacated".

When the Bank was cleared, a decree was issued by Negrin demanding the surrender of gold held by private individuals within a certain number of days, under heavy penalties. Gold objects of inestimable value have been stolen from bank safes, churches, institutions and private houses, and sold at a fraction of their value.

The Spanish Reds, indeed, have made no secret of the fact, already well proven by their actions, that their aim was to make Spain a Soviet dependency.

General Franco, on the other hand, has made it abundantly clear that not one inch of Spanish soil shall ever be yielded. His determination in this regard has rallied the patriotic youth to his side. Those who imagine that Franco will allow himself to be used by any country to further its aims, after the war of liberation, do not know the character of the man.

Nationalist Spain in any case is in no way alarmed about these prophecies, and is perfectly content in the knowledge that there is no more likelihood of Italy or Germany making any claim for Spanish territory than there was of the U.S.A. or Britain claiming the French territory they occupied during the Great War.

Italy and Germany are assisting Franco solely in their own interests; so, too, are France and Russia assisting the Reds. Britain is similarly concerned—it is the concern of all—with the

Mediterranean. The little Irish group were the only foreign participants who had no selfish motives.

Franco will make no compromise; there can be only one end to the war: complete victory for the Nationalist Army—and this is in sight. If Russia and France withdrew their support from the Reds, Franco would agree at once to the withdrawal of Italy and Germany. As I have shown already, he would never have accepted foreign aid in the struggle had Russia and France not poured in their troops and munitions in aid of the Reds.

As recently as February, 1938, Sir Henry Page Croft, British M.P., said: "How can we speed up the withdrawal of Italians when a flood of fighting men are crossing the French frontier into Spain, and Russia is sending in vast supplies of munitions."

Even since then, in March and April, there is abundant evidence on the one hand that not only war materials but daily supplies of food are being transported across the frontier from France to Catalonia; and on the other hand, Italy asserts that not a single man or gun has left Italy for Nationalist Spain in 1938, and Germany has long since ceased to send support. Germany's assistance was at all times confined to technical units, such as engineers, wireless and anti-aircraft experts.

Were it not, as I have stated, for the intervention of Russia and France, Franco would have won the war in the first month, notwithstanding the fact that all the advantages were on the Red side. As a Government, they were in a position, through their diplomatic agencies, to get the ear of the world, and to spread propaganda on a lavish scale. They had control of the public services, of the public purse, of the banks and the police. They controlled the arms and munitions stores at Madrid and Barcelona, and the factories and textiles were in their hands. Franco's officers found it difficult to procure even a useful map of Spain, for the Government controlled, of course, the Ordnance Survey Department at Madrid.

Today, Franco has a huge army of loyal soldiers, well organised, highly trained, and experienced. The official bulletins issued from Nationalist headquarters give truthful accounts of the defeats and of successes alike—there is no boasting. On the other hand, the Reds are becoming demoralised and disintegrated. Their least little advance is hailed as the forerunner of early victory; but when the Nationalist forces advance, President Negrin appeals to France and England for aid.

The Nationalist victory in the Asturias crowned all previous successes. It shortened the Nationalist front by two hundred miles, it released a force of over fifty thousand men, it gave Franco an immense amount of war material, five munition factories, and control of the principal mining and industrial parts of Spain.

Chapter XX

OUR DUTY DONE

THE IRISH BRIGADE had now fulfilled its obligations. One of the conditions was that the period of service should be for the duration of the war or for six months—November 1936 to May 1937—whichever would be the shorter. There was, of course, no contract entered into, but it was necessary to name a time limit, and it was believed then that the war would be over in six months at the latest. In fact, because of the many disappointments and postponements it was feared that it would be over by the time we got there.

Many volunteers had been able to make arrangements with their employers to have their positions kept open to them for six months, and about the end of April over a hundred officers, N.C.O.'s and men, made application to return to Ireland in May. In all cases they expressed their willingness to remain until the bandera was returning if that was my desire.

Other causes were tending also to weaken the bandera numerically. Representations had been made to General Franco by the Free State Government, through the Irish Minister in Spain, indirectly, and by the British Government through their Ambassador in Lisbon, also to me direct by this Ambassador, and by solicitors and clergy acting for the next of kin—to have a number of minors returned.

General Franco told me that when the minors were claimed by their Governments he considered they should be repatriated. On a scrutiny it was found that there were over one hundred legionaries under twenty-one years of age; but not one of them desired to go home before the others, though pressure from Ireland was being maintained.

We had also one hundred and twenty men in hospitals suffering from wounds, shell-shock, rheumatic fever, pulmonary diseases, and through an outbreak of typhoid fever. In addition to those killed in action, others had succumbed to maladies incidental to the campaign.

Even at the outset the effective strength of the bandera had been one hundred and fifty below the official establishment strength of a bandera in the Spanish army.

Yet, in the belief that we would have at least a reserve bandera I had guaranteed before the volunteers left Ireland—having received a definite assurance from the Spanish authorities—that the Irish units would be maintained as such, and officered by Irishmen. Without a reserve it was now impossible for us to continue as a distinct Irish unit, and following the passing of the Irish Non-Intervention Act we were confronted with the position that all hopes of a reserve had vanished.

Ten thousand Irishmen had responded to my call for volunteers, but we had been unable to transport them to Spain. We had no ships of our own. We had not Government resources behind us as in Italy and Germany, France and Russia; and Spain had not a ship to spare.

The volunteers in the trenches eagerly awaiting news of support from the homeland, had learned instead that they were outlawed by the home Government, a bill having been rushed through the Dáil, making it a criminal offence, punishable by the most drastic penalties, to facilitate their comrades in joining them. Half an hour after the Bill had been passed a proclamation had been issued putting it into immediate operation.

While all this was going on, hundreds of young Irishmen had been crossing to England to join the British Army without

let or hindrance. Nothing wrong was seen in their going to fight
for His Britannic Majesty—perhaps against the Indians or the
Arabs in Palestine—but it was made a crime to go from Ireland
to fight for Christ the King. Those who died for the Faith in
Spain, however, will have an abiding place in the memory of
the Irish people when those who outlawed them have been forgotten.

When I discussed the matter with General Franco and his
staff, they fully appreciated the position. We could now entertain no hope of a reserve, and as the bandera, in its depleted
condition, with consequent limitation of action, could no longer
be effectively maintained as an exclusively Irish unit—a commitment to which I was bound to adhere—there was no alternative but to disband it as such.

It was agreed that those who desired to remain in the legion
for the duration of the war should have an opportunity of doing
so, and that those who desired to return to Ireland should be
repatriated. Accordingly I arranged to meet the various platoons
and I put the position before them as fairly and impartially as I
could, making it clear that each volunteer was free to decide for
himself, and that those who elected to remain would have the
good wishes of those who elected to return.

Six hundred and fifty-four volunteers decided to return and
nine decided to remain. Of these latter, two had only just arrived
in Spain, and two returned to Ireland almost immediately afterwards.

Notwithstanding the hardships they had endured; though
they were run down generally, and were all in need of medical
attention, a rest and a change of clothing; though their duties
were doubled consequent upon the large proportion in hospital;
and though they felt very keenly aggrieved over the action of the
home Government in prohibiting a reserve from coming to their
support, the spirit and morale were as high on their last day in
the trenches as on the first. They knew no fear. If I had called
upon them to take Madrid they would have died cheerfully in
the attempt.

Every man would have agreed at once to remain had I so urged. They deplored the circumstances which prevented them from participating in the final and victorious battle in the cause for which they had volunteered. Greater loyalty no leader ever enjoyed. I know they appreciated my efforts on their behalf, but I was unable to do half as much for them as they deserved.

Cáceres, where the bandera was trained, was also the repatriation centre, and here, with splendid food, a change of clothing, bathing facilities, good sleeping quarters and peaceful surroundings, the men soon recuperated. All except eight were able to travel home with the general body. Nurse MacGorisk and Nurse Mulvaney very kindly agreed to remain in Cáceres to continue their good work for the wounded and sick, and since then all have been able to return.

Before leaving Cáceres, all the members of the Brigade met, and an association was formed "to perpetuate the name of the Irish Brigade, and the ideals and principles for which our comrades died and for which all have made sacrifices; to arrange to bring home the bodies of our martyrs, and to organise a day of national commemoration; to provide for the dependents of the members who were killed or incapacitated; and to secure employment for and safeguard the interests of the members generally." A Brigade Council representative of each of the thirty-two counties of Ireland was elected. The Association is strictly non-political.

General Franco wrote me:

"I shall always hold a grateful memory of the young Irishmen who for the justice of our cause did not vacillate in offering their services, and their lives, and many made sacrifices in defence of the high ideal that animates the Spanish people in the fight for the independence of the Fatherland and for Christian civilisation against Moscow Communism.

"Accept, my dear General, my feelings personally for yourself, and which I also extend to all the brave men of the

Irish Brigade. With this I also express my sympathy for, and salute the noble Irish people for the moral support they gave to National Spain.

"I send you my affection. May God give you many years."

The Bishop of Cáceres, the Military Governor, the Mayor, the chiefs of the army medical and other special services, the heads of the Felange and Requetes—all either wrote or called on me at the Hotel Alvarez, which had been my headquarters while in Spain, to express regret at our departure, and gratitude for our support.

I travelled to Salamanca to say "goodbye" to Very Rev. Dr. A. J. McCabe, formerly of the Diocese of Kilmore, and now Rector of the Irish College in Salamanca, and to thank him for his hospitality, not only to myself, but to all members of the Brigade who visited the world-renowned college. A perfect host, he possesses a remarkable knowledge of Spain and the Spanish people. He visited the bandera while it was in training at Cáceres, and preached an impressive sermon; he was very disappointed that the bandera should have found it necessary to leave. The Vice-Rector at Salamanca College is Father O'Hara of the Diocese of Elphin. With two such faithful guardians, the interests of Ireland are in safe keeping at General Franco's headquarters.

I also met again Señor Sangroniz, the hardworking, efficient and courteous chief of the Diplomatic Department, who had interested himself in the Irish Brigade from the beginning.

General Franco gave orders that one of the best ships on the sea should be procured to bring home the Irish Brigade, that the catering should be first-class fare, and that a special first-grade train should be engaged to convey the Brigade to Lisbon, at a total cost of £8,000. His generous action was only consistent with his kindness from the day we had arrived in Spain.

Responsibility for giving effect to General Franco's orders was entrusted to Staff Captain Fernando Camino, who represented him on my staff. No more capable officer could have been selected; he had a first-class record on the field, was an able administrator, and it was a compliment to the Irish bandera when General Franco acceded to my request, and to the Captain's own request, that he should be appointed on my staff.

One of the first to make application to join the bandera was Captain Arturo O'Ferrall, native of Dublin. He had command of a company of the Requetes on the Northern Front, and because of the bravery he displayed on the field his commanding officer was very reluctant to part with him.

At La Maranosa Captain O'Ferrall was our bandera adjutant, and later was my private secretary. He speaks seven languages fluently, but he is only happy when leading a company in the front fighting line.

The Captain was permitted to remain in Cáceres until the last of our sick and wounded were certified as fit to travel home.

Owing again to the unavoidable exigencies of the war, a Spanish ship which had been detailed for the transport of the Brigade was called up for service with the Navy at short notice. This caused us all much disappointment.

Captain Camino and myself then travelled to Lisbon, and made terms with a well-known English travel agency for a special ship. At the last moment this arrangement was cancelled for some unexplained reason. Eventually, after much fruitless negotiation with various shipping companies, we succeeded, through the good services of an influential friend of the Brigade and of Ireland, Senhor Pedro Lancastra of Lisbon, in completing a contract with the Companhia Nacional de Navegacio, of Portugal, for the hire of their six-thousand-ton liner, the *Mozambique*, for a voyage from Lisbon to Dublin.

The ship having been chartered, many other essentials then had to be attended to, some of which presented what appeared to be almost insuperable difficulties. We had to locate and transfer the sick and wounded from the various hospitals to Cáceres;

to make provision for those unable to travel home; to procure clothing and travelling requisites; to have pesetas exchanged for sterling; arrange for special trains from Cáceres to the Portuguese frontier and thence across Portugal to Lisbon, for meals on train, border customs, luggage; prepare a timetable to ensure arrival in Dublin at a fixed hour.

The *Mozambique* was only licensed to carry four hundred passengers, and additional sleeping quarters had to be prepared to the satisfaction of the Board of Trade; arrangements had to be made for meals in relays; for the quantity and quality of food, for an English-speaking medical officer, and for medical supplies. Embarkation duty and Lisbon port fees, which amounted to hundreds of pounds, were entirely unforeseen, and necessitated a bank draft from Dublin. It was necessary also to get an assurance from the Free State Government that there would be no difficulty about disembarkation in Dublin, and the shipping company required a guarantee before leaving Lisbon that demurrage for any undue delay in the Port of Dublin would be paid, also harbour dues, port fees, pilot's fees, hire of a tender if necessary, and particulars regarding the depth of water in river, at wharf, et cetera, et cetera.

It was a time of much anxiety for me, with the possibility always of a further hitch in the arrangements at the last moment, because of circumstances over which I had no control. I was a tired but happy man when the *Mozambique* sailed out of Lisbon docks at 10 p.m. on 17th June, 1937.

Senhor Lancastra's services were invaluable. With the Portuguese Government, with the Board of Trade, with the shipping company, with the banks, he was always able to set the wheels in motion. Without him I never could have overcome the problems which confronted me.

The Portuguese Minister for Finance, Dr. Jans de Costa Leite, whom I met, conveyed greetings from Dr. Salazar, the Prime Minister, and from the Government. Dr. Leite interested himself personally in all our requirements. I should also express our thanks to Senhor Van der Burgh, Senhor A. D. Bello and Captain Bothelo for their kind assistance.

The last Spanish officer to bid us farewell before we crossed the frontier into Portugal was Lieutenant Mariano Arecheder-rata, the popular Paymaster and Administration Officer to the Irish bandera. This book would be incomplete if I did not pay him a well-deserved tribute. He was courteous and diligent, and one of the most efficient officers I met in Spain. Not only did he look after the pay and allowances of all ranks, but he co-operated wholeheartedly in regard to commissariat generally.

From the arrival of the first volunteer in Cáceres, Lieutenant Arechederrata was unremitting in his attention to our require-ments, and he accompanied the bandera to the frontier on the homeward journey, to personally supervise the catering, and to ensure that each man would be provided with rations for the long train journey across Portugal to Lisbon.

On behalf of the bandera I tender to him our appreciation and gratitude.

We had a very pleasant four-day sea voyage in excellent weather. The ship's staff, from the captain down, left nothing undone in providing for our comfort, and all the volunteers seemed to enjoy the trip. As a special tribute to the Brigade, Conde de Seisal, and Senhor M. Pinto of Lisbon, sons of the Directors of the Line, accompanied us to Dublin on the *Mozam-bique*.

On the third day at sea, I received a radiogram from Dublin to the effect that the Government had received a message from Lisbon, signed "Well-wisher," that there was typhus fever among the passengers on board the *Mozambique*, and that the Dublin civic authorities were alarmed. The message received by the Government was false and mischievous, but I found it nec-essary to produce a clean bill of health, signed by the captain and the ship's medical officer.

The *Mozambique* sailed into Dublin Bay about mid-day on June 22nd, and was met in the harbour by Dr. Russell, Medical Officer of Health, and other medical officials. After a thorough examination Dr. Russell reported: "There is not a single case of sickness on board. I made an inspection of the ship and found everything in hygienic condition. All the volunteers are in an excellent state of health and the captain and ship's surgeon gave me a good medical report."

The ship then drew in alongside the quay and the men disembarked. They were accorded a memorable reception by the citizens of Dublin. Over ten thousand people had assembled at the quays, having waited there from early morning. Headed by the St. Mary's Pipers' Band, which had accompanied us to Spain, and the Tramway Workers' Band, the Brigade marched off to the Mansion House. Thousands lined the quays and O'Connell Bridge, traffic was held up, and at the Mansion House the dense crowd broke through the police cordons. From the steps of the Mansion House the Lord Mayor, Alderman Alfred Byrne, T.D., welcomed the Brigade home.

After refreshments a reception was held in the Round Room, at which the Right Rev. Monsignor Waters, P.P., V.F., presided, and an address of welcome was read by Captain Liam Walsh. The Rev. Chairman, the Lord Mayor, Alderman White (Mayor of Clonmel), Lord Ffrench, Dr. Delaney (Longford), Colonel Butler (Tipperary), P. Belton (Chairman Dublin County Council), Dermot O'Sullivan, father of Major O'Sullivan, all addressed the meeting, and after I had replied on behalf of the Brigade, the volunteers left for home with their relatives and friends.

Our little unit did not, because it could not, play a very prominent part in the Spanish war, but we ensured that our country was represented in the fight against world Communism. The guilt which might justly be ascribed to Ireland in days to come has been mitigated by the Brigade offering. Our very presence on the Madrid front focussed attention on the significance of the struggle, and showed where the sympathy of the bravest and best Irish hearts lay.

Our volunteers were not mere adventurers. Over ninety per cent, were true Crusaders, who left behind them comfortable homes—many left secretly, lest anything should arise to prevent them carrying out their resolve. They were not mercenary soldiers. Every man made a real personal sacrifice in going to Spain, and every one returned poorer in the world's goods. Many have been refused their former positions again, and are still unemployed. They are undismayed because, as they proved so well in Spain, they are men of spirit and merit.

We have been criticised, sneered at, slandered, but truth, charity, and justice shall prevail, and time will justify our motives. We seek no praise. We did our duty. We went to Spain.

INDEX

August 2019
Reconquista Press
www.reconquistapress.com

Lightning Source UK Ltd.
Milton Keynes UK
UKHW021308081220
374817UK00012B/2586